Farrago Latina

farrāgō ~inis, *f.* a medley

A Teacher Resource

GAYLAN DUBOSE

and a list of resources by

JUDITH LYNN SEBESTA

Bolchazy-Carducci Publishers, Inc.
Wauconda, Illinois

L & L Enterprises
Algonquin, Illinois

General Editor
Laurie Haight Keenan

Contributing Editors
LeaAnn Osburn
Thalia Pantelidis Hocker

Cover Design
Charlene Hernandez

Bolchazy-Carducci Publishers, Inc.
1000 Brown Street, Unit 101
Wauconda, IL 60084

ISBN 0-86516-398-7

and

L & L Enterprises
2408 Dawson Lane
Algonquin, IL 60102

Printed in the United States of America
2001
by United Graphics

Library of Congress Cataloging-in-Publication Data

DuBose, Gaylan, 1941-
Farrago latina : a teacher resource / Gaylan DuBose and a list of resources by Judith Lynn Sebesta.
p. cm.
Includes bibliographical references (p.).
ISBN 0-86516-398-7 (pbk. : alk. paper)
1. Latin language—Study and teaching (Secondary)--Aids and devices. 2. Latin language--Grammar--Problems, exercises, etc. I. Sebesta, Judith Lynn. II.Title.
PA2063.D83 1997
478.2'421--dc21 97-34993
CIP

Table of Contents

Chapter One: Some First and Probably Some Onlies 1
Famous and Infamous Facts from Roman History

Chapter Two: Stained Glass Windows 4
An Art Project Based on Latin Grammar

Chapter Three: Some Surprising Connections 11
Relationships between Various Aspects of Ancient and Modern Cultures

Chapter Four: What Some Latin Words Really Meant 16
A Study of Meanings Based on Indo-European Roots

Chapter Five: Perīculum Latīnum 23
An Answer and Question Game

Chapter Six: *Nox, Mox, Mons* and *Mens* Driving Kids Out of Their Minds 58
A Successful Sequence for Teaching Words Commonly Confused

Chapter Seven: Making the *Aeneid* a Matter for Focused Reading 64
Specialties for the *Aeneid*

Chapter Eight: Certamina 71
Certamen Rounds for All Levels of Latin

Chapter Nine: Endings 96
A Study of Endings Common to More Than One Form

Readings and Resources 99
by Judith Lynn Sebesta

Acknowledgments

I began writing the forerunner of this book in 1994 when two people close to me were dying. I dedicate my work, then, to the memory of Theresa Collings and Robert Beebe. I thank the late Marian Patricia Felts, my English professor for four semesters at the University of North Texas, for suggesting that I minor in Latin. I give special thanks to Lea Ann Osburn, my editor and friend throughout this process, and to Thalia Hocker, who helped in so many ways. Diane Smith deserves special thanks for formatting the text as do the Bolchazys for having the confidence to publish my work. I thank my brother, Joe, who gave me my first computer, without which I never would have begun all this, and all my students over the years for their support and inspiration. Finally, I thank Frank Franklin and Don Ischy for their constant support, interest in this project, and friendship.

About the Author

Gaylan DuBose earned a Bachelor of Arts Degree with high honors in English at the University of North Texas and a Master of Arts Degree in Classics from the University of Minnesota. He taught Latin and English for thirty-two years before retiring in May 1997. He remains actively involved in Junior Classical League at the area, state and national levels. He lives in Austin, Texas, and is currently working on two other books.

Chapter One

Some Firsts and Probably Some Onlies

The items in this chapter contain the kind of information many of my students find interesting. I often put this type of information on the chalkboard as something for the students to copy into their notebooks while I check the roll and sign absentees permits. Later in the period we discuss other information about the individuals mentioned in the item. The items can later form *certamen* questions for in-class competitions or can be "tested" as extra credit items on quizzes or tests. Policies regarding the use of extra credit on tests vary from school to school and even from department to department within a school. Learn the policy and abide by it.

I cannot stress enough the importance of having something on the chalkboard for the students to copy into their notebooks every day. Having something to do lets them know from the beginning of the period—and indeed from the beginning of the year—that they are in the Latin room to learn and to work. Of course, we also have fun. Sometimes I put mottoes or historical facts or dates on the chalkboard. Beneath the focus item, I always list the objectives and activities for that day. Of course, experienced teachers know about the importance of this information's being available to the students; however, I hope first-year teachers may benefit from this advice.

The first

...king of Rome: .... **Romulus**

...Roman to have a triumph: .... **Romulus**

...emperor of Rome: .... **Gaius Julius Caesar Octavianus, later Augustus**

...Julio-Claudian emperor: .... **Gaius Julius Caesar Octavianus, later Augustus**

...Arabian to become emperor: .... **Philippus**

...emperor to die while hiding in a latrine: .... **Elagabalus**

...plebeian to become emperor: .... **Septimius Serverus**

...emperor to profess to be a Christian: .... **Constantine**

...emperor to be Christian: .... **Constantius**

...emperor to embrace Christianity fully: .... **Theodosius**

...Illyrian emperor: .... **Claudius II**

...emperor to participate in a triumph in women's garb: .... **Elagabalus**

...Bishop of Rome: .... **(St.) Peter**

...Christian martyr: .... (St.) Stephen

...Roman to commit fratricide: .... Romulus

...wife of Gaius Julius Caesar: .... Cossutia

...wife of Aeneas: .... Creusa

...Roman hill to be settled: .... the Palatine

...Roman to give names to the months: .... Numa Pompilius

...Consuls: .... Brutus and Collatinus

...source of Latin: .... the Praeneste fibula

...Roman to employ dactylic hexameter: .... Ennius

...aqueduct: .... the Aqua Appia

...province of Rome: .... Sicily

...triumvirate: .... Caesar, Crassus and Pompey

...triumph of Gaius Julius Caesar: .... ex Gallia

...Flavian emperor: .... Vespasian

...Roman emperor to appear with a beard: .... Hadrian

...calendar published showing Christian & pagan holidays including December 25 as Christmas and the feast of the unconquerable sun: .... A.D. 354

Chapter Two

Stained Glass Windows

One activity which my students have enjoyed and which I consider educationally worthwhile is the coloring of what I call Roman Stained Glass Windows or *Fenestrae Romanae.* Many students need to discriminate between the meanings, forms, or part of speech of various Latin words. *Fenestrae Romanae* are designed to accomplish this objective while providing a classroom or homework activity which is different from the more usual types. A nice by-product of this activity is colorful papers with which to decorate the Latin room or to show to parents during conferences or at open houses. In addition, there are extension activities which may be used after a class finishs a set of *Fenestrae Romanae.* Artistically talented students may wish to design their own *Fenestrae Romanae.*

There are five *Fenestrae Romanae* on the following pages. The first two focus on the parts of speech and the meanings of Latin vocabulary words and are designed for the beginning student but may be used at any level. The third contains nouns of all five declensions but no irregular nouns are included. The fourth contains examples of all indicative tenses in the active and passive voices, but no irregular verbs are used. The fifth illustrates indicative and subjunctive verb forms in all tenses, and both voices and irregular verbs are included.

In order to maximize the effectiveness of these activities, the teacher should conduct a classroom review of the topic contained in the window and identify for the students any vocabulary items which are not familiar. Coloring instructions are included on each window page but it is usually helpful if the teacher reads the instructions aloud and asks if there are any questions.

After the students complete the coloring of the chosen *Fenestra Romana,* consider using one of the following extension activities. One extension activity is to direct the students to choose five words out of the window and to find synonyms and/or antonyms for these five words. Another extension activity is to ask the students to find English derivatives for a selected number of words in the window. A third extension activity is to instruct the students to replace each word in the window or a selected number of words in the window with another Latin word which is in the same form or category. Finally, mount the colored *Fenestrae Romanae,* if possible, in the classroom and enjoy!

Coloring Instructions for the parts of speech in the fenestra above: Color nouns *red*, verbs *green*, adjectives *blue*, adverbs *yellow*, prepositions *purple*, pronouns *pink*, conjunctions *brown*, and interjections *orange*. If a space is blank, you may color it as you choose.

Coloring Instructions for the nouns in the fenestra above: Color the name of people *blue*, the names of things *red*, the names of ideas or qualities *yellow*. If a space is blank, you may color it as you choose.

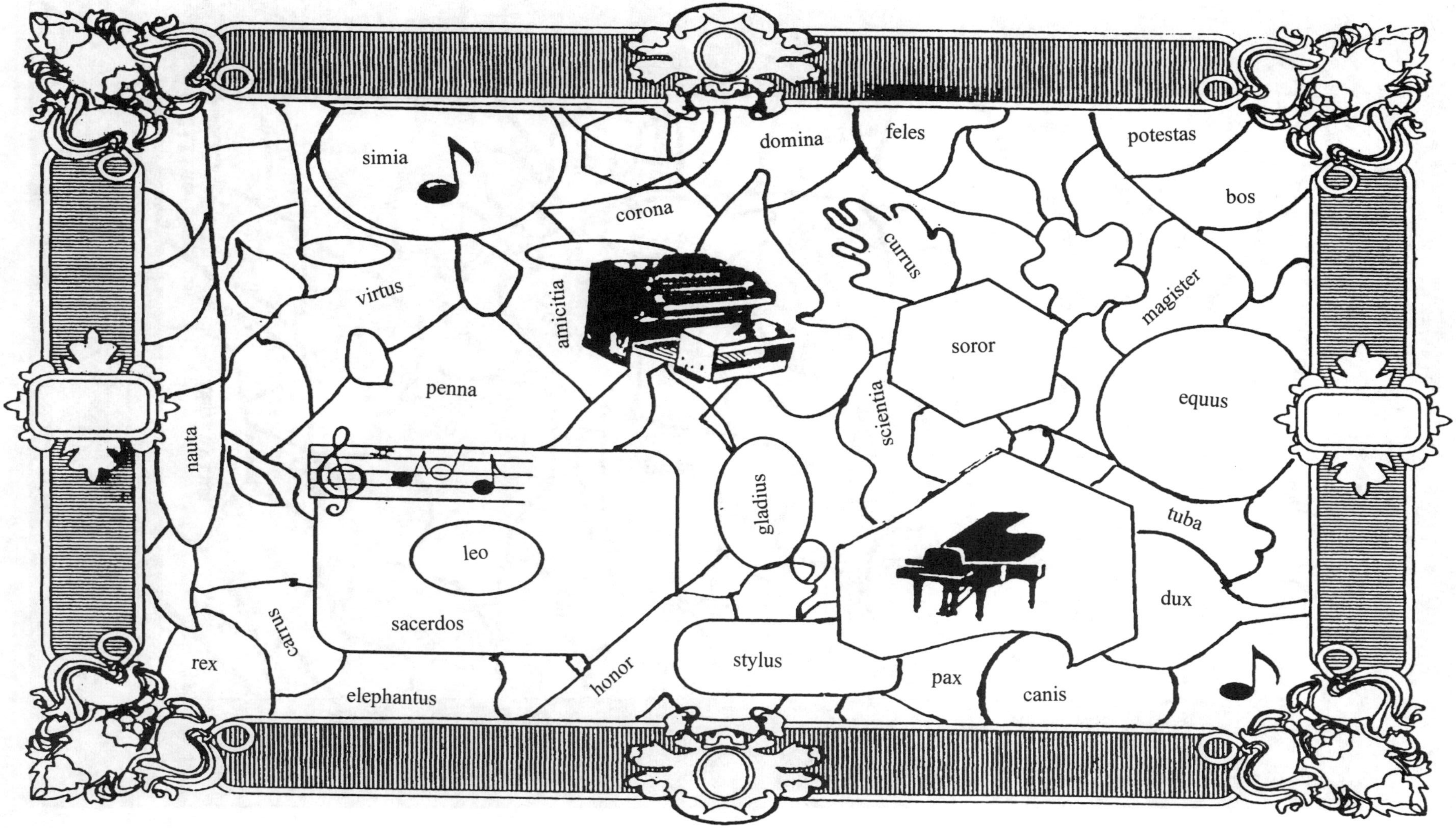

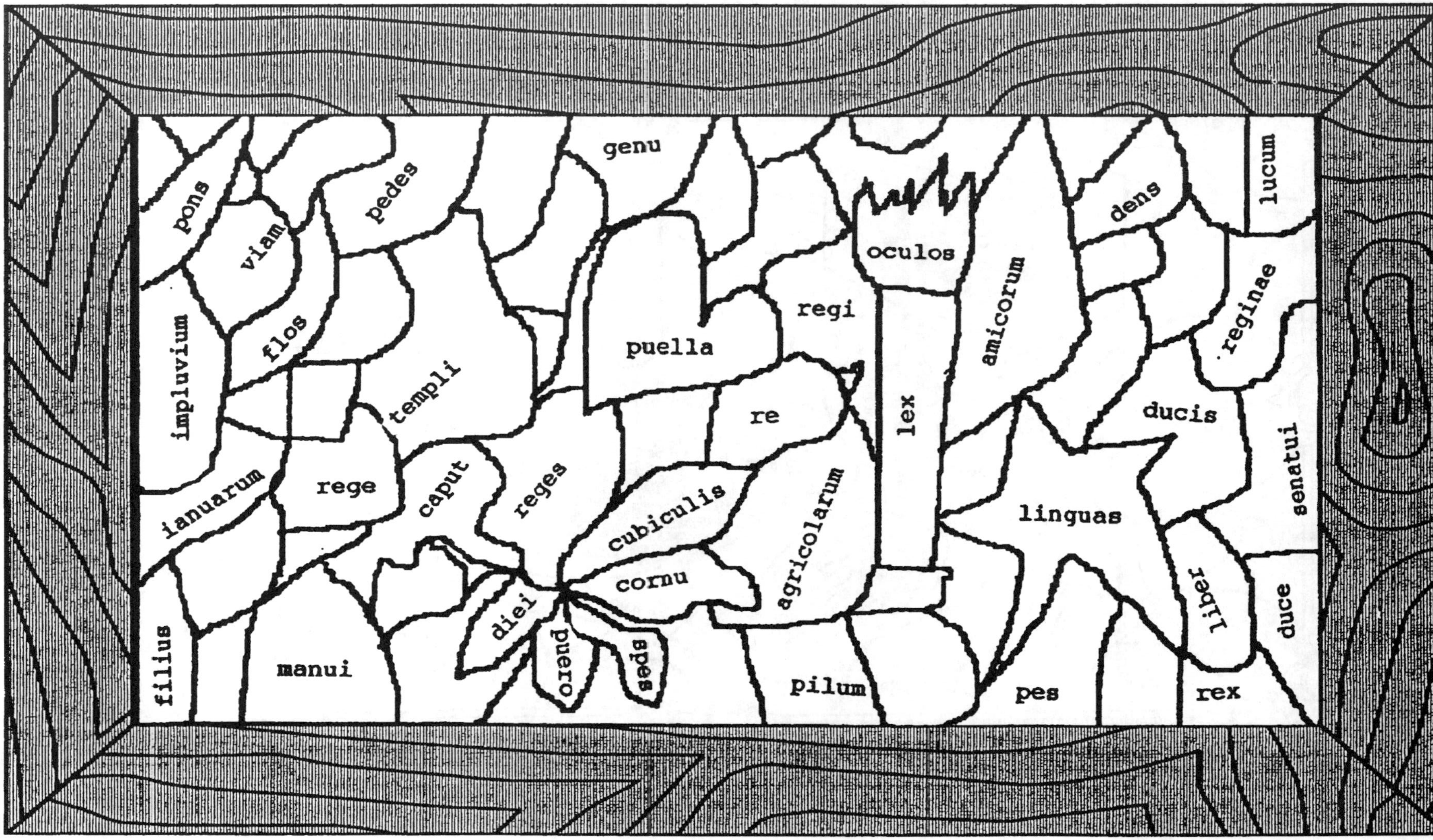

Coloring Instructions for the nouns in the fenestra above: Color the nominative *red*, genitive *blue*, dative *green*, accusative *yellow*, and the ablative *purple*. If a noun can be more than one case, color its space *pink*. If a space is blank, choose any color you like.

Coloring Instructions for the verbs in the fenestra above: Color the present tense *red*, the imperfect *blue*, the future *green*, the perfect *orange*, the pluperfect *yellow*, and the future perfect *purple*. If a space is blank, choose any color you like.

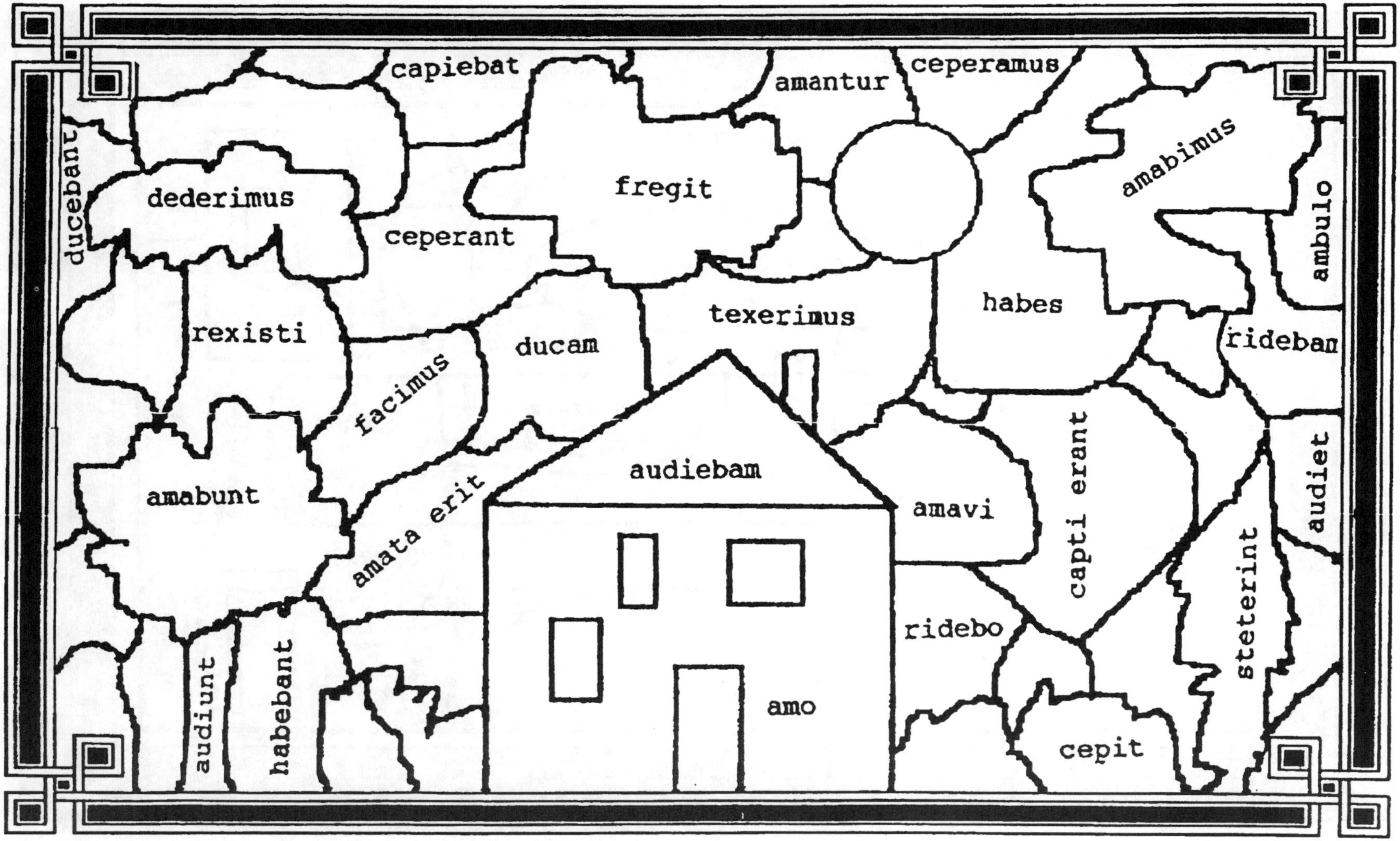

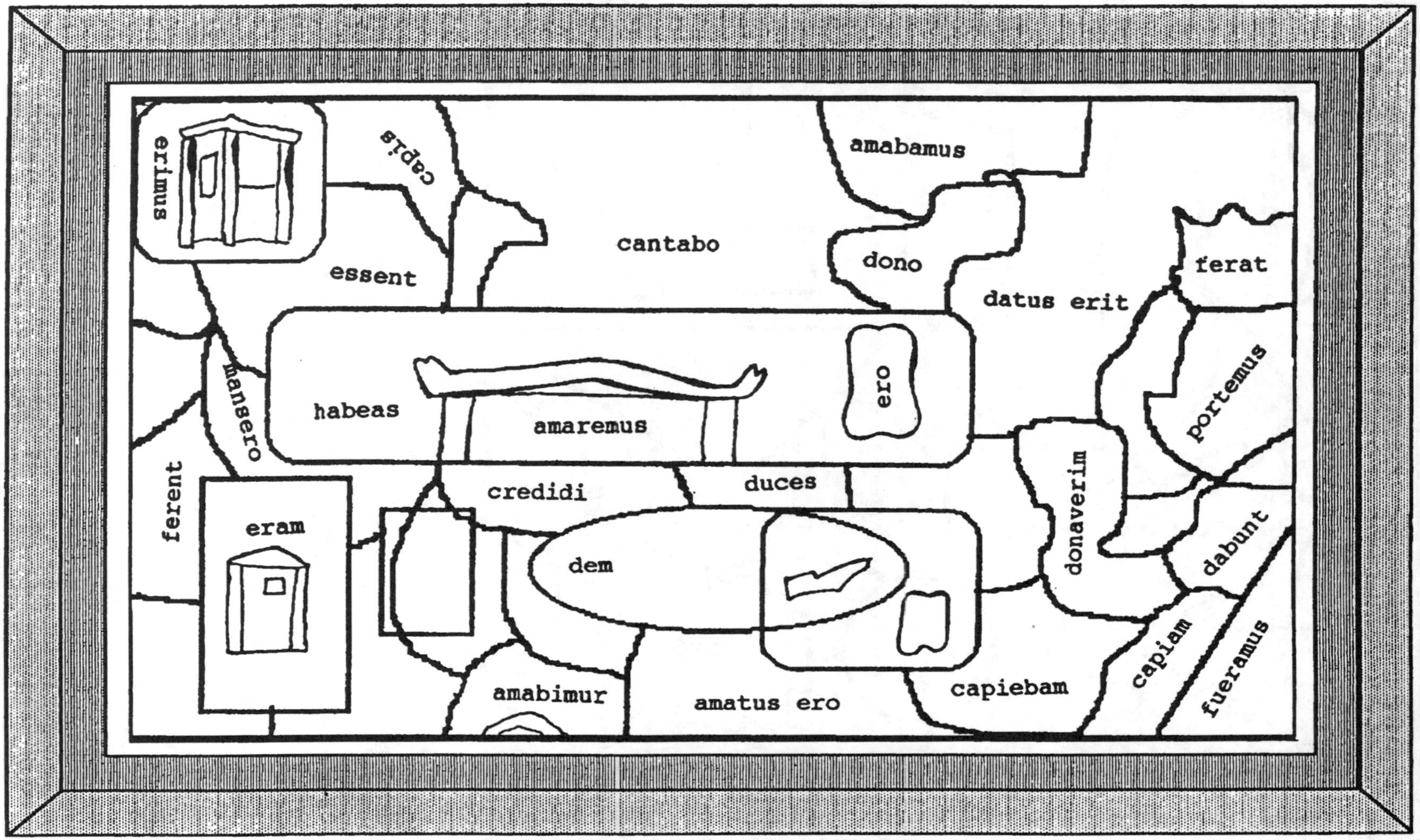

Coloring Instructions for the verbs in the fenestra above: Color the present tense *red*, the imperfect *blue*, the future *green*, the perfect *orange*, the pluperfect *yellow*, and the future perfect *purple*. If a verb may be more than one tense, color its space *pink*. If a space is blank, choose any color you like.

Chapter Three

Some Surprising Connections

Recently I was half-way watching a program on some cable channel. I looked up momentarily to see a baby animal of some kind in Australia (I don't know what it was.) being licked into shape by its mother. We had just been reading the eighth book of the *Aeneid*, and I was immediately reminded of the following lines:

Fecerat et viridi fetam Mavortis in antro
procubuisse lupam, geminos huic ubera circum
ludere pendentes pueros et lambere matrem
impavidos, illam tereti cervice reflexa
mulcere alternos et corpora fingere lingua.
Book VIII, lines 630–635

And he had made the newly-delivered she-wolf lying in Mars' green grove, and hanging around her teats twin boys were playing, and the mother wolf was licking the fearless boys; having bent her smooth neck, she caressed them in turn and shaped their bodies with her tongue.
Tr. Gaylan DuBose

I had often spoken of licking my students into shape, but I thought that usage referred to licking with a strap or rod in the old days. I know now that it really does allude to the way it was believed new-born animals were licked into shape by their mothers' tongues. There are other surprising connections which I have found and attempted to explain in this chapter. A student exercise sheet follows the explanations.

A salary was originally an allowance for Roman soldiers to use to buy salt. But did you know that the most important ingredient in a salad was considered to be the salt? The Italian word for salad, *insalata*, literally means "ensalted" or "salted on." In the same way, an enchilada is literally something "chilied on."

Did you ever wonder why we use "'s" to show possession? Consider the genitive ending for third declension: -*is*. Just as Latin had *homo, hominis* to mean "man, man's/ of the man," Old English had *man, manniz*. As time went on, British speakers often dropped aitches (h's) but also inserted them where they didn't belong. And so *manniz* eventually became "man his," as in "the man his field." Then the aitch (h) dropped out to become "man'is." You can guess the next step: "man'is" became "man's" just the way "cannot" became "can't." In your English class you may come across "The Lord Chamberlain his Men." And at one time, the proper expression was not "The Queen of England's Crown" but "The Queen's Crown of England." (I'll bet at one time there was an expression like "the queen his crown," but I can't prove it.)

And now about plants. I was amazed that the word pansy comes originally, by way of the frequentive *penso*, from the Latin *pendo*, which means "weigh, pay, hang." Now if you think about it, when you think, you weigh different possibilities. As Shakespeare, who, as Norah Lofts said to me once, knew everything, wrote in *Hamlet*, pansies are for thoughts. The French word for thoughts is *pensées*. So pansies. (Consider also *pensive*.) So much for that, but I was aghast to learn that a connected word is spider, because a spider is really a spinner, and spin and the Latin *pendo* are from the same root. "You could look it up."

An *arbor vitae*, called in Texas an "arbor vida" (rhymes with Ida) and in the Midwest an "arbor vidy" (rhymes with tidy) is really the tree of life. It's an evergreen, of course. Ironically, in the South, these trees are seen most often in cemeteries, much as cypress trees are in Italy. I used to think that whoever named the plant *ficus Benjamina* didn't know much about Latin. I was the ignorant one, though, because I hadn't yet learned that the names of most trees are second declension feminine.

One famous dynasty of England, by way of France, was the Plantagenet family. The name of this super-aristocratic family merely means "broom plant," *planta genestra* in Latin. While speaking of French things, let us pause to remember that dandelion means "tooth of the lion," coming as it does from the French *dens de leon* from the Latin *dens leonis*.

And now to foods we go. *Cabbage* comes from a Latin word meaning "head." The word *unus* gave us our word onion and a radish is merely a root (Latin *radix*). Bean comes from an Indo-European root *bha-bha*, which means "broad bean" or any bean. The root became *faba* in Latin. You might want to research Grimm's Law to find out why. (I can't tell you everything, you know!)

A popular dish in most of the United States is usually called "chili." Its full name is *chile con carne*, which means "chili with meat." *Chili* is powdered pepper, and *carne* is derived from the Latin *caro, carnis*, meaning of flesh. So really we call this dish by the less substantial but more important ingredient in the recipe.

Names of some other foods whose names are derived from Latin are *pork*, from *porcus*, which means "pig" and veal. Veal is from the Latin *vitulus* or *vitellus*, calf. Can you see the connection to the name Vitellius (Roman Emperor, A.D. 69)? The Indo-European root from which we derive veal is *wet-* and means "year"; hence a yearling. The root also gives the Latin *vetus*, old, having many years. I have a strong suspicion that Italy is from the same root, since the Latin *Italia* is derived from the Oscan *Viteluit*. Veal to this day is a popular meat in Italy.

Texas was the first state to adopt the standard gauge railroad track statewide. The standard gauge track has the rails as far apart as the wheels were on a Roman chariot: 4' 8.5". And that's the truth!

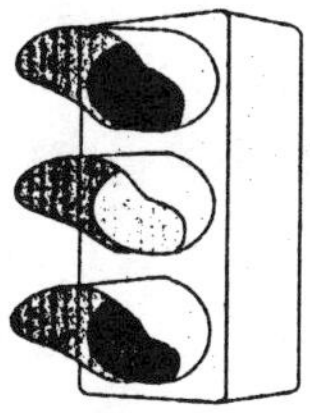

Even the expression "jay-walk" goes back to Late Latin. The Late Latin *gaius* meant a foolish or inexperienced person, or a newcomer. So a person who jay-walks is either a fool or has no experience with big-city traffic. Also, a jay is a foolish bird.

The name of two parts of the body have surprising connections to other words. To my knowledge, *caput* is the only Latin noun ending in *-ut*. *Ut* means, of course "as." Caput means literally "cup-like." That connection is not hard to see; however, the same root for *caput*, head, also gives us "tub." I had always thought that "have" is derived from *habeo*. Recently, though, I learned that it is from *capio*. If you seize something, you have it. Surprisingly, *hand* also comes from the same root as *capio* and "have." Your hands, then, are your seizers. (When I told my Latin IV students this fact, one of them quoted Hamlet's "pickers and stealers!").

Some Surprising Connections

Exercise IIIa

Check what you have learned about Latin words and their meanings by completing the following matching exercise.

__________	1. homo	A. salt
__________	2. dens	B. broom plant
__________	3. faba	C. pig
__________	4. gaius	D. calf
__________	5. caput	E. tongue
__________	6. porcus	F. bean
__________	7. sāl	G. a foolish person
__________	8. lingua	H. man
__________	9. vitellus	I. head
__________	10. planta genestra	J. tooth

Exercise IIIb

Find four Latin words in Chapter Three which are written in the genitive singular case.

1. ______________________
2. ______________________
3. ______________________
4. ______________________

Exercise IIIc

How well did you read? Find out with this *Verum aut Falsum* exercise based on Chapter Three.

_____ 1. The wheels on a Roman chariot were 4', 8.5" apart.
_____ 2. The Italian word *insalata* has the same Latin root at its base as the Spanish word *enchilada*.
_____ 3. The Latin word *ficus* is second declension feminine.
_____ 4. *Manniz* is an old English word in the genitive singular.
_____ 5. Pansies, pensive, and spider are all from the same Latin root word.

Key to Exercises in Chapter Three

Exercise IIIa

1.	H	6.	C
2.	J	7.	A
3.	F	8.	E
4.	G	9.	D
5.	I	10.	B

Exercise IIIb

Words in the genitive case

Mavortis
hominis
vitae
leonis
carnis

Exercise IIIc

True—False

1. Verum
2. Falsum
3. Verum
4. Verum
5. Verum

Chapter Four

What Some Latin Words Really Meant

One day recently my Latin II class was reading Caesar; and, when we came to the part about the discovery of Orgetorix' daughter and one of his sons in the Helvetian camp, one of my students asked why those two words (*filia* and *filius*) were alike. I reminded him of their English "meaning," but he said,"I know; but what does the root mean?" I had never thought about that and didn't know, but I vowed to find out. In order to find out—and this is what your students need to do for the exercise included below—I looked up *filial* in the dictionary. The derivation information gave a root. When I looked in the appropriate appendix, I was amazed to learn that the root means "suck." The word *filius*, then, must originally have meant just "the [male] one who sucks." My students were as fascinated with this information as I was and said, "What about some other words, DuBie?" I suggested they give me some common Latin words, and they suggested *femina*. Lo and behold! It really meant "she who gives suck."

I decided not to tell my students that any Latin word really means any English word. Rather we've been saying that the Romans used, for example, *amo* to signify the same emotion we signify by *I love*. This idea has helped us to realize that Latin words had many different connotations to the Romans and there is a hardly ever a one-to-one transfer of "meaning."

So, on to some more words and suggestions. Anyone who has taught Latin any time at all knows how students love the word *facio*, especially because of its present imperative singular. Naturally, they wanted to look up *facio*. Its root means "do." Interestingly enough, the root became the Latin *facio*, but it also entered Latin as the *-dos* in *sacerdos*; hence the *sacerdos* was the "doer of the holy." The root came into English, of course, as *do*.

We learned also that *mater* is from the baby talk *ma* plus the suffix of relationship *-ter*. (Consider also *matertera*.) Nothing earth-shaking there, but connected to *mater* is *materia* because wood comes from the trunk, or *matrix*, of the tree.

I hope your students will enjoy this research as much as mine have. All the words listed in the exercise are ones my students and I found to be interesting, but I'm sure your students will come up with their own favorite words, too.

What Some Latin Words Really Meant

Exercise IVa

In order to complete this exercise, you will need a dictionary with an appendix containing roots or with root meanings given at the dictionary entry. A good dictionary with an appendix containing roots is *The American Heritage Dictionary of the English Language: High School Edition*. First, look up a derivative of the Latin word. In the dictionary mentioned above, the first derivative of the Latin word will indicate the root from which the Latin word comes. Second, look up the root in the appendix (if it is not given with the entry, depending upon what dictionary you are using). Third, write down the "real" meaning of the Latin word according to its root. Finally, write down at least two other English words related to the Latin word or other Latin words related to the original Latin word.

Example: nauta (sailor):
Root and Root Meaning: ____nau____ = ____boat____
Meaning of the Latin Word According to its Roots: ____boat person____
Other English Words Derived From The Same Root ____navigate, nausea____

1. **puer** (boy)
Root and Root Meaning: ________________ = ________________
Meaning of the Latin Word According to its Roots: ________________
Other English Words Derived From The Same Root: ________________

2. **animal** (animal)
Root and Root Meaning: ________________ = ________________
Meaning of the Latin Word According to its Roots: ________________
Other English Words Derived From The Same Root: ________________

3. **aedificium** (building)
Root and Root Meaning: ________________ = ________________
Meaning of the Latin Word According to its Roots: ________________
Other English Words Derived From The Same Root: ________________

4. **forum** (forum)
Root and Root Meaning: ________________ = ________________
Meaning of the Latin Word According to its Roots: ________________
Other English Words Derived From The Same Root: ________________

5. **vir** (man)
Root and Root Meaning: ________________ = ________________
Meaning of the Latin Word According to its Roots: ________________
Other English Words Derived From The Same Root: ________________

6. **dux** (leader, general)
Root and Root Meaning: ____________________ = ______________________________
Meaning of the Latin Word According to its Roots: ______________________________
Other English Words Derived From The Same Root: ______________________________

7. **amō** (I love)
Root and Root Meaning: ____________________ = ______________________________
Meaning of the Latin Word According to its Roots: ______________________________
Other English Words Derived From The Same Root: ______________________________

8. **vērus** (true)
Root and Root Meaning: ____________________ = ______________________________
Meaning of the Latin Word According to its Roots: ______________________________
Other English Words Derived From The Same Root: ______________________________

9. **vetus** (old)
Root and Root Meaning: ____________________ = ______________________________
Meaning of the Latin Word According to its Roots: ______________________________
Other English Words Derived From The Same Root: ______________________________

10. **māter** (mother)
Root and Root Meaning: ____________________ = ______________________________
Meaning of the Latin Word According to its Roots: ______________________________
Other English Words Derived From The Same Root: ______________________________

Now, choose **three of your own favorite Latin words** and follow the same procedures.

1. ____________________(____________________):
Root and Root Meaning: ____________________ = ______________________________
Meaning of the Latin Word According to its Roots: ______________________________
Other English Words Derived From The Same Root: ______________________________

2. ____________________(____________________):
Root and Root Meaning: ____________________ = ______________________________
Meaning of the Latin Word According to its Roots: ______________________________
Other English Words Derived From The Same Root: ______________________________

3. ____________________(____________________):
Root and Root Meaning: ____________________ = ______________________________
Meaning of the Latin Word According to its Roots: ______________________________
Other English Words Derived From The Same Root: ______________________________

Then look up the following English words and do the same: **brother, sister, tong, dental.**

What Some Latin Words Really Meant

Key to Exercise IVa

E.g. Root: *nau-* = boat "boat person." Other words: navigate, nausea, French *nacelle*

1. Root: *pou-* = little or few, variant form: *pu* = boy, child "little one." Other words: paraffin (that which produces little), pauper, paucity. (From variant form *pulo* = young of an animal: pullet [Latin *pullus* = chick], pony, foal)
2. Root: *ane-* = breathe "that which breathes." Other words: unanimous, girl's name Enid (soul), animosity
3. Root: *aidh-* = burn "burning place/hearth." Other words: aedile, edifice, Latin *aestas* (summer)
4. Root: *dhwer-* = door or **dhwor-ans* (alternate form Latin *foras*) "out of doors/outside." Other words: forest, foreclose, forfeit
5. Root: *wiros-* = man or *wei-* = vital force "forceful/strong one." Other words: Latin *curia<co-vir* (men together), violent, violate
6. Root: *deuk-* = lead "leader." Other words: tug, duke, educate
7. Root: *amma-* = various nursery words, including the meaning of *mother.* Other words: girl's names Mabel, Emily, amicable, amateur
8. Root: *weros-* = true "true." Other words: warlock, girl's name Veronica, very, French *voir dire*, severe
9. Root: *wet-* = year "person with years." Other words: yearling, wether (a neutered goat, as in *bell wether*, the wether with the bell who leads the flock), veterinarian, veal, veteran
10. Root: *ma-* = mother + -ter = suffix of relationship "ma relative." Other words: matrix, material

Extra Words to Look Up:

1. Root: *bhater-* = brother "brother or fellow member of a clan." Other words: friar, fratricide, fraternal, brother, brotherhood
2. Root: *swesor-* = sister "sister." Other words: Latin *soror* (sister), Latin *sobrinus* (maternal cousin), sorority, sisterhood
3. Root: *denk-* = bite "biting thing." Other words: tenacious, Latin *teneo* (hold), Latin *tenax* (tough)
4. Root and Root Meaning: *dent-* = tooth "tooth-like." Other words: tusk, orthodontist, tooth

N.B. Not all the other English words derived from the same root have been included. The connections are many and fascinating!

What Some Latin Words Really Meant

Exercise IVb

First, look up a derivative of the Latin word. In *The American Heritage Dictionary of the English Language: High School Edition*, for example, the first derivative of the Latin word will indicate the root from which the Latin word comes. Second, look up the root in the appendix (if it is not given with the entry, depending upon what dictionary you are using). Third, write down the "real" meaning of the Latin word according to its root. Finally, write down at least two other English words related to the Latin word or other Latin words related to the original Latin word.

Example: nauta (sailor):
Root and Root Meaning: ____**nau**____ = ____**boat**____
Meaning of the Latin Word According to its Roots: ____**boat person**____
Other English Words Derived From The Same Root ____**navigate, nausea**____

1. **mensa** (table)
Root and Root Meaning: ____________ = ____________
Meaning of the Latin Word According to its Roots: ____________
Other English Words Derived From The Same Root: ____________

2. **ōvum** (egg)
Root and Root Meaning: ____________ = ____________
Meaning of the Latin Word According to its Roots: ____________
Other English Words Derived From The Same Root: ____________

3. **oculus** (eye)
Root and Root Meaning: ____________ = ____________
Meaning of the Latin Word According to its Roots: ____________
Other English Words Derived From The Same Root: ____________

4. **toga** (toga)
Root and Root Meaning: ____________ = ____________
Meaning of the Latin Word According to its Roots: ____________
Other English Words Derived From The Same Root: ____________

5. **salus** (health)
Root and Root Meaning: ____________ = ____________
Meaning of the Latin Word According to its Roots: ____________
Other English Words Derived From The Same Root: ____________

6. **horridus** (horrid)
Root and Root Meaning: ____________________ = ______________________________
Meaning of the Latin Word According to its Roots: ______________________________
Other English Words Derived From The Same Root: ______________________________

7. **ventus** (wind)
Root and Root Meaning: ____________________ = ______________________________
Meaning of the Latin Word According to its Roots: ______________________________
Other English Words Derived From The Same Root: ______________________________

8. **folium** (leaf)
Root and Root Meaning: ____________________ = ______________________________
Meaning of the Latin Word According to its Roots: ______________________________
Other English Words Derived From The Same Root: ______________________________

9. **stramentum** (straw)
Root and Root Meaning: ____________________ = ______________________________
Meaning of the Latin Word According to its Roots: ______________________________
Other English Words Derived From The Same Root: ______________________________

10. **canis** (dog)
Root and Root Meaning: ____________________ = ______________________________
Meaning of the Latin Word According to its Roots: ______________________________
Other English Words Derived From The Same Root: ______________________________

What Some Latin Words Really Meant

Key for Exercise IVb

1. Root: *me-* = to measure "measure/time for a meal." Other words: month, moon
2. Root: *awi-* = bird "bird thing/egg." Other words: ostrich, avine
3. Root: *okw-* = to see "little seeing thing." Other words: daisy, inoculate, Latin *atrox* = black looking
4. Root: *steg-* = to cover "cover/covering thing." Other words: protect, thatch
5. Root: *sol-* = whole "wholeness." Other words: catholic, salvation, solid, solidarity
6. Root: *shers-* = bristling "caused to bristle (as the hair on end)." Other words: hedgehog, urchin, caterpillar
7. Root: *we-* = to blow "blowing thing." Other words: weather, Nirvana
8. Root: *bhel-* = to blow/bloom/swell "thrive, bloom/round thing." Other words: boll, girl's name Phyllis, chlorophyll, bull
9. Root: *ster-* = to spread "spread/spread thing." Other words: structure, industry, street, sternum
10. Root: *kwan-* = dog "dog." Other words: cynic, hound, Canary Islands

Chapter Five

Periculum Latinum

Classroom learning games are good experiences for students and can enliven the classroom. *Periculum Latinum,* like the popular television show "Jeopardy!," supplies answers in five categories for which the students gain points by giving the correct question. At the novice and intermediate levels of *"Periculum Latinum,"* the five categories are Latin grammar, mythology, Latin vocabulary, derivatives, and Roman history/life. At the advanced level, the five categories are the same but Latin literature is included in the mythology category. Teachers across the United States have developed their own rules and methods for this learning game. Below is a method which works well, and following these pages there are ten rounds of *"Periculum Latinum"* questions at each of the three levels.

Instructions:

1) Make transparencies of the following four pages.
2) Place the transparency for *"Periculum Latinum"* from whichever level you choose to play onto an overhead projector.
3) Lay a plain transparency on top of the *"Periculum Latinum"* transparency. As each value is attempted, write an "x" over that category with a washable transparency pen.
4) Form teams of four. Use the Quiz Wizard set so that anyone on any team may buzz in, not locking out members of the same team.
5) Read aloud the answers from the pages labelled *"Periculum Latinum: Answers & Questions."*
6) Allow consultation only <u>before</u> a team member has signalled. Allow no consultation for a team after a member of that team has signalled. Other teams may consult until a member signals.
7) Award points when a correct question is given and subtract points for an incorrect question.
8) After all the questions in the *"Periculum Latinum"* round have been used, remove the *"Periculum Latinum"* transparency and place the transparency *"Periculum Duplicatum"* on the overhead. Continue as described above, reading answers from a different page until all answers have again been used. **N.B.** On the question pages all questions are labelled 100, 200, etc. While this is

correct for the "*Periculum Latinum*" round, in the "*Periculum Duplicatum*" round the teacher should when reading each question double the amount from 100, 200 etc. to 200, 400, etc.

9) You may include a round of "*Periculum Ultimum*" by asking each team to wager an amount of points and by then reading an answer from the "50 Extra Answers" page. Allow one minute for each team to write a question for this final answer on a piece of paper. Add the amount wagered for each team that wrote the correct question and subtract the amount wagered for an incorrect answer.

10) The team with the most points wins the game.

Perīculum Latīnum

Grammar	Mythology	Vocabulary	Derivatives	History/Life
100	100	100	100	100
200	200	200	200	200
300	300	300	300	300
400	400	400	400	400
500	500	500	500	500

Novice & Intermediate

Perīculum Duplicātum

Grammar	Mythology	Vocabulary	Derivatives	History/Life
200	200	200	200	200
400	400	400	400	400
600	600	600	600	600
800	800	800	800	800
1000	1000	1000	1000	1000

Novice & Intermediate

Perīculum Latīnum

Grammar	Myth/Lit	Vocabulary	Derivatives	History/Life
100	100	100	100	100
200	200	200	200	200
300	300	300	300	300
400	400	400	400	400
500	500	500	500	500

Advanced

Perīculum Duplicātum

Grammar	Myth/Lit	Vocabulary	Derivatives	History/Life
200	200	200	200	200
400	400	400	400	400
600	600	600	600	600
800	800	800	800	800
1000	1000	1000	1000	1000

Advanced

Quaesita Periculo Latino
Novice Level

Categories are as follow: GRAMMAR, MYTHOLOGY, VOCABULARY, DERIVATIVES, and ROMAN HISTORY AND LIFE

[N.B. Please notice that questions are repeated in different forms so that the teacher can determine whether or not the students are learning from playing the game.]

Round One

GRAMMAR

100:	There are this many declensions of nouns.	What is five?
200:	There are this many conjugations of verbs.	What is four?
300:	This case is used to show by what means something is done.	What is the ablative?
400:	This verb tense shows the earlier of two actions both in the past.	What is the pluperfect?
500:	This principal part gives the present stem.	What is the second (principal part)?

MYTHOLOGY

100:	He is the Roman god with two faces.	Who is Janus?
200:	Hercules performed this many labors.	What are twelve?
300:	She is the mother of Proserpina.	Who is Ceres?
400:	These are the daughters of Zeus and Mnemosyne.	Who are the Muses?
500:	She turned Arachne into a spider.	Who was Athena/Minerva?

VOCABULARY

100:	This Latin word means "farmer."	What is *agricola?*
200:	This Latin word means "country estate."	What is *villa?*
300:	This is the third principal part of *sum.*	What is *fui?*
400:	This is the genitive of *civis.*	What is *civis?*
500:	This is the gender of *mare.*	What is neuter?

DERIVATIVES

100:	This Latin word gives us *library.*	What is *liber?*
200:	This Latin word is the origin of *peddle.*	What is *pes?*
300:	*Auditorium* comes from this Latin verb.	What is *audio?*
400:	This is the meaning of the derivative *amicable.*	What is *friendly?*
500:	This Latin derivative means "a foot and a half long."	What is *sesquipedalian?*

HISTORY AND LIFE

100:	Chariot races were held in these.	What were circuses?
200:	She wore the *tunica recta.*	Who was the bride?
300:	This was the main meal of the day.	What was *cena?*
400:	He was the Roman king who established religion at Rome.	Who was Numa Pompilius?
500:	He was Rome's greatest orator.	Who was Cicero?

Round Two

Grammar

100:	These cases are used for the object of *in.*	What are the accusative and ablative?
200:	This case is the case used most of the time to show possession.	What is the genitive?
300:	This is the nominative and accusative plural of *lux.*	What is *luces?*
400:	This is the gender of *nauta.*	What is masculine?
500:	There are this many declensions of adjectives.	What is three?

Mythology

100:	She was turned into a spider.	Who was Arachne?
200:	According to the Romans' religion, everything had one of these.	What were *numina?*
300:	She became merely a voice crying in the wilderness.	Who was Echo?
400:	He made wings for himself and his son.	Who was Daedalus?
500:	He was the only imperfect and ugly diety.	Who was Vulcan/Hephaestus?

Vocabulary

100:	This is the third principal part of *pono.*	What is *posui?*
200:	This Latin word means "I sail."	What is *navigo?*
300:	This Latin word is an antonym of *malus.*	What is *bonus?*
400:	This Latin word is a synonym of *laetus.*	What is *felix/beatus/fortunatus?*
500:	This Latin word means "head."	What is *caput?*

Derivatives

100:	This derivative from Latin literally means "brotherhood."	What is *fraternity*?
200:	This Latin word is at the root of *radish.*	What is *radix?*
300:	This Latin verb gives us the girl's name Emily.	What is *amo?*
400:	This Latin word for "red" gives us *ruby.*	What is *rubrus?*
500:	This derivative describes one who receives benefits.	What is a *beneficiary*?

History and Life

100:	He was the emperor when Jesus was born.	Who was Augustus?
200:	This fell in A.D. 476.	What was the Western Roman Empire?
300:	This was the original name of the Colosseum.	What was the Flavian Amphitheatre?
400:	This was the name of the first dynasty of emperors.	What was Julio-Claudian?
500:	He was the emperor when Jesus was crucified.	Who was Tiberius?

Round Three

Grammar

100:	This tense shows action done habitually in the past.	What is the imperfect?
200:	This case is used for indirect objects.	What is the dative?
300:	This is the fourth principal part of *dono.*	What is *donatus/donata/donatum?*
400:	This is the genitive of *amicus.*	What is *amici?*
500:	This is the gender of *poeta.*	What is masculine?

Mythology

100:	He was Venus' son and the god of love.	Who was Cupid?
200:	He was Cupid's father.	Who was Mars?
300:	He carried Persephone into the underworld.	Who was Hades?
400:	He was the youngest of the gods.	Who was Dionysus/Bacchus?
500:	He had a lock of purple hair.	Who was Nisus?

(cont.)

VOCABULARY

100: This is the third principal part of *do*. — What is *dedi?*
200: This is the third principal part of *sto*. — What is *steti?*
300: This declension contains the word *ager*. — What is the second (declension)?
400: This declension has a sub-class called "i-stem." — What is the third (declension)?
500: This is the gender of *cornu* and *tonitru*. — What is neuter?

DERIVATIVES

100: This Latin noun, the name of a part of the body, gives us *sequipedalian*. — What is *pes?*
200: This Latin verb gives us the words *count* and *compute*. — What is *puto?*
300: This Latin adjective gives us *difficult*. — What is *facilis/difficilis?*
400: This Latin adverb is at the beginning of *malefactor*. — What is *male?*
500: This Latin verb gives us the Spanish verb *hacer*. — What is *facio?*

HISTORY AND LIFE

100: His name means "Little Boots" or "Bootsie." — Who was Caligula?
200: His twin founded Rome. — Who was Remus?
300: He attempted to found a city on the Aventine Hill. — Who was Remus?
400: The bride wore this type of tunic. — What was the *tunica recta*?
500: He was the fifth Julio-Claudian emperor. — Who was Nero?

Round Four

GRAMMAR

100: This syllable denotes the first person singular, future tense, active voice for first and second conjugation verbs. — What is *-bo-?*
200: This syllable shows the third person plural, imperfect tense, active voice. — What is *-bant?*
300: This voice shows that the subject is acted upon by an agent. — What is the passive (voice)?
400: This is the passive form of *amatis*. — What is *amamini?*
500: This is the ablative plural of *dea*. — What is *deabus?*

MYTHOLOGY

100: This hero completed tasks assigned by Eurystheus. — Who was Hercules/Heracles?
200: She was the mother of Aeneas. — Who was Venus?
300: This Greek god's bird was the eagle. — Who was Zeus?
400: He ferried the dead across a river in the underworld. — Who was Charon?
500: This is the river of forgetfulness. — What is the Lethe?

VOCABULARY

100: One of these words means "I have" and the other means "I live in" or "I dwell." — What are *habeo* and *habito?*
200: This word means "way," "street," or "road." — What is *via?*
300: This word has the genitive plural of *pontium*. — What is *pons?*
400: This word means "home." — What is *domus?*
500: This word is a first conjugation verb meaning "I rule." — What is *regno/regnare?*

DERIVATIVES

100: This is the meaning of the Latin verb which gives us *convention?* — What is "come"?
200: This Latin verb meaning "I find" gives us *invention*. — What is *invenio?*
300: This Latin word gives us *duke* and *duchess*. — What is *dux* or *duco?*
400: This derivative means "one who does evil." — What is *malefactor*?
500: This derivative of *vir* means "manly." — What is *virile*?

(cont.)

HISTORY AND LIFE

100: She was the mother of Romulus and Remus. Who was Rhea Silvia?
200: This emperor's name means "lame" or "crippled." Who was Claudius?
300: The Roman Empire reached its greatest territorial extent under this emperor. Who was Trajan?
400: Senators wore shoes of this color. What is red?
500: A boy received this object on the ninth day of his life. What is a *bulla?*

Round Five

GRAMMAR

100: Of these words this one does not belong with the others because of a point of grammar: *eram, portabam, ero,* and *poteram.* What is *ero?*
200: This is the tense of *ero.* What is the future?
300: This is the tense of *eram.* What is the imperfect?
400: *Habeo* is in this conjugation. What is the second (conjugation)?
500: *Corpus* is in this declension. What is third (declension)?

MYTHOLOGY

100: This creature was half man and half bull. What was the Minotaur?
200: The peacock was this goddess' bird. Who was Juno/Hera?
300: He carried the bident. Who was Hades/Pluto?
400: He had a donkey's ears and a special touch. Who was Midas?
500: This creation helped to bring about the downfall of Troy. What was the wooden/Trojan horse?

VOCABULARY

100: Of these words, this one does not belong because of its meaning: *canis, porcus, leo,* and *cena.* What is *cena?*
200: Of these words, this one does not belong because of its meaning: *tigris, canis, felix,* and *bos.* What is *felix?*
300: This word means "kingdom" or "royal power." What is *regnum?*
400: This word's genitive is *regis.* What is *rex?*
500: This word means "unfriendly" or, as a noun, "a personal enemy." What is *inimicus?*

DERIVATIVES

100: This Latin adverb gives us *benefactor* and *beneficiary.* What is *bene?*
200: This word derived from *malus* is used to describe a bad growth in the body. What is *malignant*?
300: This Latin noun is the origin of *vital* and *vitamin.* What is *vita?*
400: This Latin noun meaning "help" gives us *auxiliary.* What is *auxilium?*
500: This Latin name for a domestic animal gives us *vaccine.* What is *vacca?*

HISTORY AND LIFE

100: He was the last of the Julio-Claudian emperors. Who was Nero?
200: He succeeded Trajan as emperor. Who was Hadrian?
300: Of these, this is a beverage a Roman would never have drunk: beer, coffee, wine, or milk. What is coffee?
400: This is what the Romans called breakfast. What is *ientaculum?*
500: This was what a Roman schoolboy wrote with. What was a *stylus?*

Round Six

Grammar

100: This is the case used to show accompaniment. What is the ablative?
200: This tense shows the earlier of two actions, both in the future. What is the future perfect?
300: This is the name of the symbol used to mark a vowel long. What is a macron?
400: This is the name for the next to the last syllable of a word. What is the penultimate?
500: Of these words, one does not belong because of a point of grammar: *flos, mons, senatus,* and *tempus.* What is *tempus*?

Mythology

100: She was the Greek counterpart of Diana. Who was Artemis?
200: He had an oracle at Delphi. Who was Apollo?
300: She turned Tithonus into a grasshopper. Who was Aurora/Eos?
400: Of these, she alone is not a virgin goddess: Venus, Vesta, and Diana. Who was Venus?
500: This animal killed Adonis. What is a wild boar?

Vocabulary

100: This is the Latin adverb formed from *clarus.* What is *clare?*
200: This is the Latin adverb formed from *acer.* What is *acriter?*
300: This Latin word means "break." What is *frango?*
400: This is the genitive of *corpus.* What is *corporis?*
500: This is an antonym of *felix.* What is *infelix/miser?*

Derivative

100: This derivative from Latin means "sail around." What is *circumnavigate*?
200: Of these, one is not derived from *lux*: translucent, luxurious, and lucidity. What is *luxurious*?
300: This derivative from Latin means literally "carried across." What is *transported/ translated/transferred*?
400: This noun gives us *delapidated.* What is *lapis?*
500: This is the meaning of *bilateral.* What is two-sided/having two sides?

History and Life

100: Romans did this in the *triclinium.* What is eating/dining?
200: This toga was worn by one seeking political office. What is the *toga candida*?
300: A victorious general wore this type of toga. What is the *toga picta*?
400: Roman books were in this form. What is a scroll?
500: This man delivered Caesar's funeral oration. Who was Mark Antony/ Marcus Antonius?

Round Seven

Grammar

100: This is a sub-class of third declension nouns. What is i-stem?
200: Words of this part of speech modify nouns. What are adjectives?
300: This is the name of the third syllable from the end of a word. What is antepenultimate?
400: This is a syllable like *-que* attached to the end of a word. What is an enclitic?
500: This case is used for the object of the preposition *pro.* What is the ablative?

(cont.)

Mythology

100: She was the Greek goddess of agriculture. — Who was Demeter?
200: This creature is half man and half horse. — What is a centaur?
300: He is the blacksmith for the gods. — Who is Vulcan/Hephaestus?
400: He is the Roman counterpart of Poseidon. — Who is Neptune?
500: Vulcan forges armor for him in Book VIII of the *Aeneid.* — Who is Aeneas?

Vocabulary

100: This Latin word means "yesterday." — What is *heri?*
200: This Latin word means "tomorrow." — What is *cras?*
300: This is the "easy" word for Latin students. — What is *facilis/facile?*
400: This is the fourth principal of *maneo.* — What is *mansum/mansurus?*
500: This Latin word means "journey" but not "again." — What is *iter*?

Derivatives

100: This Latin noun meaning "the flowing thing" gave us *flume.* — What is *flumen?*
200: This Latin verb is at the base of *certamen.* — What is *certo?*
300: This Latin noun gives us *flower* but not *flow.* — What is *flos?*
400: This Latin verb gives us *flow* but not *floral.* — What is *fluo?*
500: This is the meaning of *cogitate.* — What is *"think"?*

History and Life

100: He was murdered on the Ides of March in 44 B.C. — Who was (Gaius Julius) Caesar?
200: This was the date of the Battle of Actium. — What was September 2, 31 B.C.?
300: She was the first wife of Augustus. — Who was Scribonia?
400: This item was discarded by a girl the night before her wedding. — What was a *bulla?*
500: This instrument was used to part the bride's hair. — What was a spear/*hasta*?

Round Eight

Grammar

100: This principal part is the present infinitive. — What is the second principal part?
200: This tense shows action completed in the past. — What is the perfect tense?
300: This is the number of declensions of adjectives. — What is three?
400: This is the dative plural of *puella.* — What is *puellis?*
500: These are the genders of third declension. — What are masculine, feminine, and neuter?

Mythology

100: She is the mother of Aeneas. — Who is Venus?
200: Odysseus' men blinded this Cyclops. — Who was Polyphemus?
300: He was the man with a thousand eyes, but not faces. — Who was Argus?
400: He was the messenger of Jupiter. — Who was Mercury?
500: He rescued Andromeda from the sea monster. — Who was Perseus?

Vocabulary

100: This is the meaning of *virtus.* — What is "courage, worth, or manliness"?
200: This is the gender of *dux.* — What is masculine?
300: This Latin word means "water." — What is *aqua?*
400: This word was Priam's title. — What is *rex?*
500: *Misi* is the third principal part of this verb. — What is *mitto/mittere?*

(cont.)

Derivatives

100: This derivative of *aqua* denotes a way the Romans obtained water from the mountains. What is *aqueduct?*
200: This Latin verb is at the root of *vivid.* What is *vivo?*
300: This Latin noun came directly into English to denote one who tells a story. What is *narrator?*
400: This Latin noun gives us a derivative to describe death by jumping down from a window. What is *fenestra?*
500: This derivative of *saxum* denotes a plant breaking through rock. What is *saxifrage?*

History and Life

100: This emperor wanted to make his horse consul. Who was Caligula?
200: This denotes a Roman citizen's given name. What is praenomen?
300: This was Gaius Caesar's *nomen.* What is Julius?
400: This man said, "*Veni, vidi, vici.*" Who was (Gaius Julius) Caesar?
500: This place was once flooded for a mock naval battle. What was the Colosseum?

Round Nine

Grammar

100: This case is used to show manner, with or without *cum.* What is the ablative?
200: This tense has the indicator of "a" or "e" for third and fourth conjugation verbs. What is the future?
300: This is the name given to two vowels which produce one sound. What is a diphthong?
400: This is the Latin name for the last syllable of a word. What is ultima?
500: Of these words, one does not belong because of a point of grammar: *veniam, amabo, duco, regam.* What is *duco?*

Mythology

100: His oracle gave messages through the rustling of oak leaves. Who was Zeus?
200: She is the Roman goddess of the hunt. Who is Diana?
300: He ruled during the golden age on earth, according to the Romans. Who was Saturn?
400: She is the Roman goddess of fruit. Who is Pomona?
500: A female animal of this type was Zeus' nurse. What is/was a goat?

Vocabulary

100: This Latin word is the adjective form of *alte.* What is *altus/a/um?*
200: This Latin word has *tactus* as its fourth principal part. What is *tango?*
300: This is the gender of *corpus* and *flumen.* What is neuter?
400: This Latin word means "lucky," "fortunate" or "successful." What is *felix?*
500: This Latin verb, like *dico,* means "I say." What is *inquam?*

Derivatives

100: This Latin adjective gives us the name of one who always looks for or sees the best. What is *bonus/optimus?*
200: This Latin noun gives us *fidelity.* What is *fides?*
300: This is the literal meaning of the derivative *umbrella.* What is "little shade"/ "little shadow"
400: This Latin adjective gives us *acrimonious.* What is *acer?*
500: This word means "put off until tomorrow." What is *procrastinate?*

(cont.)

History and Life

100: This is the name for the spirit which the Romans believed was in absolutely everything. — What is the *numen?*
200: A Roman girl might become a Vestal Virgin at this age. — What is six?
300: This was the business and social center of ancient Rome. — What was the Forum?
400: This king of Rome bought the Sybilline books. — Who was (Lucius) Tarquinius Superbus?
500: Remus saw this many vultures in the sky when he and Romulus were trying to decide what to name their new city. — What is six?

Round Ten

Grammar

100: This conjugation has a sub-class called *-io.* — What is the third (conjugation)?
200: This conjugation has a long "e" in its second principal part. — What is the second (conjugation)?
300: The indicators for this tense in first conjugation verbs are *-bo, -bi,* and *-bu.* — What is the future tense?
400: This is the name given to such syllables as *-ne, -que,* and *-ve.* — What is enclitic?
500: The adjective *acer* has this many terminations. — What is three?

Mythology

100: Hercules performed these many labors. — What are twelve?
200: He was sired by Zeus in the form of a golden shower. — Who was Perseus?
300: This couple was instructed to throw their mother's bones behind them. — Who were Deucalion and Pyrrha?
400: She was turned into a cow, but Hera was still suspicious. — Who was Io?
500: She was turned into a sunflower. — Who was Clytie?

Vocabulary

100: This Latin word means "house," "hut," or "cottage." — What is *casa?*
200: This Latin word means "home." — What is *domus?*
300: This is the second principal part of *duco.* — What is *ducere?*
400: This is the genitive of *civis.* — What is *civis?*
500: This is the gender of *nomen.* — What is neuter?

Derivatives

100: The word *amateur* comes from this Latin verb. — What is *amo?*
200: This Latin noun gives us *vitamin.* — What is *vita?*
300: This Latin verb is the basis of *currently.* — What is *curro?*
400: *Extraterrestrial* comes from this Latin noun. — What is *terra?*
500: If we *illuminate* something, we give it this. — What is light?

History and Life

100: This was the master's study in a *domus.* — What is the *tablinum?*
200: This was used to divide a bride's hair into locks. — What was a spear/*hasta*?
300: The Western Roman Empire fell in this year. — What was A.D. 476?
400: This Roman emperor founded a city named Constantinople. — Who was Constantine?
500: This was the seaport of Rome. — What was Ostia?

Quaesita Periculo Latino
Intermediate Level

Categories are as follow: GRAMMAR, MYTHOLOGY, VOCABULARY, DERIVATIVES, and ROMAN HISTORY AND LIFE

Round One

GRAMMAR

100: This case is used for the subject of a verb. — What is the nominative?
200: This mood is used in indirect question. — What is the subjunctive?
300: This verb tense shows the earlier of two actions, both in the future. — What is the future perfect?
400: This preposition is used for the ablative of accompaniment. — What is *cum?*
500: This case is used for the subject of an infinitive. — What is the accusative?

MYTHOLOGY

100: He is the king of the Greek gods. — Who is Zeus?
200: He flew too high and melted the wax on his wings. — Who was Icarus?
300: She murdered her children to get even with her two-timing husband. — Who was Medea?
400: Replaced by Ganymede, she was the original cupbearer to the gods. — Who was Hebe?
500: He was turned into a grasshopper by Aurora. — Who was Tithonus?

VOCABULARY

100: This Latin word means "son." — What is *filius?*
200: This Latin word means "pour." — What is *fundo?*
300: This Latin word means "farmhouse." — What is *villa?*
400: This is the fourth principal part of *sterno.* — What is *stratus/a/um?*
500: This is the gender of *aequor.* — What is neuter?

DERIVATIVES

100: This Latin noun is the origin of *liberty.* — What is *libertas?*
200: This Latin noun gave us *patriotic.* — What is *patria?*
300: This Latin noun is at the heart of *cordial.* — What is *cor?*
400: This Latin noun gave us *avuncular.* — What is *avus/avunculus?*
500: This Latin cardinal number gives us *onion.* — What is *unus/a/um?*

HISTORY AND LIFE

100: He was the twin of the first king of Rome. — Who was Remus?
200: He was born in the month which now bears his name in 102 or 100 B.C. — Who was (Gaius Julíus) Caesar?
300: The Roman bride's veil was this color. — What was yellow/saffron/flame-colored?
400: These were a slave's personal savings or property. — What were *pelicula?*
500: He was the last emperor in the Western Empire. — Who was Romulus Augustulus?

Round Two

GRAMMAR

100: This case is used for the object of *credo.* — What is the dative?
200: This case is used for the object of the preposition *per.* — What is the accusative?
300: This tense shows the earlier of two actions, both in the past. — What is the pluperfect/ past perfect?
400: This case is used to show manner, as in the phrase *maximo cum studio.* — What is the ablative?
500: This Latin word introduces a positive purpose clause. — What is *ut?*

MYTHOLOGY

100: He was the master craftsman and inventor. — Who was Daedalus?
200: She became merely a voice. — Who was Echo?
300: He was turned into a partridge. — Who was Perdix?
400: She is *Eos* in Greek. — Who is Aurora/the Dawn?
500: At Juno's insistence, this minor god caused a storm perilous to Aeneas. — Who was Aeolus?

VOCABULARY

100: This Latin word means "I stand." — What is *sto?*
200: This Latin word is the antonym of *bonus.* — What is *malus?*
300: The fourth principal part of this verb is *tactus.* — What is *tango?*
400: This Latin preposition can mean "in" or "into." — What is *in*?
500: This is the gender of *manus.* — What is feminine?

DERIVATIVES

100: This Latin noun is the origin of *maternity.* — What is *mater?*
200: This Latin verb gave us *count.* — What is *puto?*
300: This is the usual ending for an English word derived from a Latin word ending in *-tas.* — What is "-ty"?
400: *Conjugal* comes from this Latin word. — What is *coniunx?*
500: This girl's name, which can be the name of a potent beverage, also means "little pearl" in Latin. — What is *margarita?*

HISTORY AND LIFE

100: This emperor believed he would conquer in a certain sign. — Who was Constantine?
200: This was Caesar's basic battle formation. — What was the *triplex acies?*
300: This was the date of the founding of Rome. — What was April 21, 753 B.C.?
400: This emperor succeeded Augustus. — Who was Tiberius?
500: He was emperor when Jesus was crucified. — Who was Tiberius?

Round Three

GRAMMAR

100: This principal part gives us the present stem. — What is the second (principal part)?
200: This principal part gives us the perfect stem. — What is the third (principal part)?
300: This tense shows action incomplete or habitual in the past. — What is the imperfect?
400: *Ab* takes its object in this case. — What is the ablative?
500: This case is used for the objects of *faveo* and *credo.* — What is the dative?

(cont.)

Mythology

100: She was the first wife of Aeneas. Who was Creusa?
200: He was king of kings and leader of the Greeks at Troy. Who was Agamemnon?
300: She was the goddess of wisdom, war, and handicrafts for the Greeks. Who was Athena/Pallas Athena?
400: This Greek god's emblem is the trident. Who is Poseidon?
500: One of her birds is the sparrow. Who is Venus/Aphrodite?

Vocabulary

100: This Latin word means "believe" in English. What is *credo?*
200: This Latin word means "I give." What is *do/dono?*
300: This is the English meaning of *mare.* What is "sea"?
400: This is the genitive of *cornu.* What is *cornus?*
500: This is the gender of *tribunal* and *cornu.* What is neuter?

Derivatives

100: This Latin word gives us the Spanish word *tiempo.* What is *tempus?*
200: The French word *mère* comes from this Latin noun. What is *mater?*
300: This Latin demonstrative adjective became the definite article in several Romance languages. What is *ille?*
400: This Latin word means "a foot and a half long." What is *sesquipedalian?*
500: This derivative of *venio* signifies a place where nuns come together. What is *convent?*

History and Life

100: He was the third Julio-Claudian emperor. Who was Caligula?
200: He was king of Rome when the Sabine women became wives to his men. Who was Romulus?
300: He was the twin brother of the first king of Rome. Who was Remus?
400: Of her sons she said, "These are my jewels." Who was Cornelia?
500: She was Caesarion's mother. Who was Cleopatra?

Round Four

Grammar

100: This case is used to show the thing with which something is done. What is the ablative?
200: This tense is indicated by "a" or "e" for third and fourth conjugation verbs. What is the future?
300: This is the tense indicator for the imperfect. What is *-ba?*
400: These Latin words introduce a negative result clause. What are *ut non?*
500: This is the genitive singular of *ipse.* What is *ipsius?*

Mythology

100: He wandered for ten years after the Trojan War. Who was Odysseus/Ulysses?
200: This was the first labor of Hercules. What was killing the Nemean lion?
300: She challenged Athena to a weaving contest. Who was Arachne?
400: He was the father of Aeneas. Who was Anchises?
500: This character gained strength every time he touched the earth. Who was Antaeus?

(cont.)

Vocabulary

100:	This Latin word means "that of yours."	What is *iste?*
200:	This is the Latin word for *sign.*	What is *signum?*
300:	This is the genitive of *virgo.*	What is *virginis?*
400:	This is the feminine form of *celer.*	What is *celeris?*
500:	This Latin word means "nothing."	What is *nihil?*

Derivatives

100:	This Latin word gives us *motor* from its fourth principal part.	What is *moveo?*
200:	This is a derivative from Latin which means an evening church service.	What is *vespers?*
300:	This derivative from Latin means a man overly protective of, fond of, or submissive to his wife.	What is *uxorious?*
400:	This Latin verb gives us *Emily.*	What is *amo?*
500:	This is the English equivalent of *trinitas.*	What is *trinity?*

History and Life

100:	She is the mother of Romulus and Remus.	Who is Rhea Silvia?
200:	This is the number of hills upon which Rome was built.	What is seven?
300:	This was the "Queen of Roads."	What was the Appian Way?
400:	These many cities were destroyed by the eruption of Vesuvius on August 24, A.D. 79.	What are three?
500:	This is the cold room in a Roman bath.	What is the *frigidarium?*

Round Five

Grammar

100:	This is the first person singular, imperfect subjunctive, active of *amo.*	What is *amarem?*
200:	This is the passive of *donat.*	What is *donatur?*
300:	This is the plural of the noun *regis.*	What is *regum?*
400:	This is the plural of *filiae.*	What is *filiarum/filiabus?*
500:	These letters indicate the pluperfect subjunctive, active.	What are "-i s s e"?

Mythology

100:	This young man fell in love with his own reflection.	Who was Narcissus?
200:	He performed twelve labors.	Who was Hercules?
300:	He is the only ugly god.	Who is Hephaestus/Vulcan?
400:	She spent half the year in the underworld.	Who was Persephone/Proserpina?
500:	Perdix was turned into this kind of bird.	What is a partridge?

Vocabulary

100:	This is the gender of *exercitus.*	What is masculine?
200:	This word does not belong with the others because of its meaning: *pes, telum, oculus, manus.*	What is *telum?*
300:	This Latin word means "foot."	What is *pes?*
400:	This is the gender of *mons.*	What is masculine?
500:	This Latin verb has the fourth principal part of *cessum.*	What is *cedo?*

Derivatives

100:	This Latin word gives us cheese and the Spanish *queso.*	What is *caseus?*
200:	This derivative of *mora* means "a delay."	What is *moratorium?*
300:	This Latin word gave us *immortality.*	What is *mors?*
400:	*Cordial* comes from this Latin noun.	What is *cor?*
500:	This derivative from *omnis* names a vehicle used for public transportation.	What is bus?

(cont.)

History and Life

100: Chariot races were held here. — What was the circus/Circus Maximus?

200: The first gladiatorial shows were probably held during this type of ceremony. — What was a funeral?

300: He was a philosopher emperor who wrote *Meditations*. — Who was Marcus Aurelius?

400: Constantine saw these words and converted to Christianity. — What were *"In hoc signo vinces"*?

500: A Roman would not have eaten one of the following: cheese, olives, tomatoes, grapes, bread. — What were tomatoes?

Round Six

Grammar

100: This is the perfect active infinitive of *do.* — What is *dedisse?*

200: This principal part is the present active infinitive. — What is the second (principal part)?

300: This is the present active participle of *venio* in the nominative singular. — What is *veniens?*

400: This case is used to show the part of a whole. — What is the genitive?

500: This case is used for indirect objects. — What is the dative?

Mythology

100: He made wondrous armor for his wife's son. — Who was Vulcan?

200: Persephone ate these in the underworld. — What are pomegranate seeds?

300: According to Greek mythology, this was the very first thing in existence. — What was Chaos?

400: She was the goat who was the nurse of Zeus. — Who was Amalthea?

500: This gorgeous man, beloved of Aphrodite, was killed by a wild boar. — Who was Adonis?

Vocabulary

100: This is the neuter form of *omnis.* — What is *omne?*

200: This Latin word means "buy." — What is *emo?*

300: This Latin word means "ship." — What is *navis?*

400: *Fractus* is the fourth principal part of this verb. — What is *frango?*

500: *Maris* is the genitive of this Latin word meaning "sea." — What is *mare?*

Derivatives

100: This Latin word gave us *marine.* — What is *mare?*

200: This stone is the color of the waters of the sea. — What is an *aquamarine*?

300: This Latin noun gave us the name of Jesus' followers. — What is *discipulus?*

400: The Latin word for teacher gave us this man's title. — What is *mister?*

500: This derivative names the pilot of a plane. — What is *aviator?*

History and Life

100: Romans dined in this room. — What is the *triclinium?*

200: The Romans believed this vegetable was a panacea, and it was Cato's favorite food. — What is cabbage?

300: This is the warm room of the bath. — What is the *caldarium?*

400: This was the characteristic dress of a Roman citizen. — What was the toga?

500: He was given the title of *Imperator* after the Helvetian campaign. — Who was (Gaius Julius) Caesar?

Round Seven

Grammar

100: This is the genitive plural of *nox*. — What is *noctium?*
200: This is the part of speech of *per, ad,* and *ex*. — What is preposition?
300: The prepostion *prae* takes this case. — What is the ablative?
400: This is the third principal part of *do*. — What is *dedi?*
500: This is the future active infinitive of *dono*. — What is *donaturus/a/um esse?*

Mythology

100: Echo turned into this. — What is a voice?
200: She greatly loved Tithonus and asked for immortality for him, but she left out a second important request. — Who was Aurora/Eos/the Dawn?
300: Homer calls her "cow-eyed." — Who is Hera?
400: Aeneas had to have this item to enter the underworld. — What is the golden bough?
500: His twin performed twelve labors. — Who was Iphicles?

Vocabulary

100: This is the genitive of *mons*. — What is *montis?*
200: This Latin word means "soon" in English. — What is *mox?*
300: This Latin word is an antonym of *vita*. — What is *mors/nex/letum?*
400: This is the English meaning of *volare*. — What is "to fly"/"to rush"?
500: This Latin word, actually meaning "a flowing thing," designates a type of body of water. — What is *flumen?*

Derivatives

100: This Latin noun meaning "the naming thing" gave us *nominate*. — What is *nomen?*
200: This derivative of *amo* means "illicit lover." — What is *paramour?*
300: This Latin adjective gave us a mathematical word for "the total." — What is *summus/a/um?*
400: This Latin verb gave us *preparatory*. — What is *paro?*
500: This Latin noun gave us derivatives naming a body of soldiers and describing a type of punishment. — What is *corpus?*

History and Life

100: He was assassinated on the Ides of March in 44 B.C. — Who was (Gaius Julius) Caesar?
200: The date of this event was April 21, 753 B.C. — What was the founding of Rome?
300: This is Gaius Julius Caesar's *praenomen*. — What was Gaius?
400: This was Marcus Tullius Cicero's *nomen*. — What was Tullius?
500: She was Julius Caesar's wife at the time of his death. — Who was Calpurnia?

Round Eight

Grammar

100: This is the nominative of *noctium*. — What is *noctes?*
200: The preposition *coram* takes this case. — What is the ablative?
300: *Alte* and *bene* are this part of speech. — What is an adverb?/What are adverbs?
400: This is the superlative of *bonus*. — What is *optimus?*
500: This is the comparative of *alte*. — What is *altius?*

(cont.)

Mythology

100: Along with the sparrow, this is also Venus' bird. — What is the swan?
200: He drove his father's chariot too close to the sun. — Who was Phaethon?
300: He was the builder of the Labyrinth. — Who was Daedalus?
400: He brought fire to mankind. — Who was Prometheus?
500: He swallowed all his children but one. — Who was Cronus?

Vocabulary

100: This is the fourth principal part of *do.* — What is *datus/a/um?*
200: This is the genitive of *reges.* — What is *regum?*
300: This is the gender of *aequor* and *mare.* — What is neuter?
400: This Latin noun means "edge," "line of battle," and "eye." — What is *acies?*
500: This Latin noun means, literally, "the struggling thing." — What is *certamen?*

Derivatives

100: This derivative naming you and a part of the eye means literally "little doll." — What is pupil?
200: This Latin noun gave us *library.* — What is *liber/librarius?*
300: This Latin verb is the root of *computer.* — What is *puto?*
400: This Latin verb gives us *direct.* — What is *dirigo/rego?*
500: This Latin noun and its meaning gave us the word *muscle,* which really means a little one of these. — What is *mus* (mouse)?

History and Life

100: The bride's hair was divided into this many locks. — What is six?
200: This garment was worn by all Romans of both sexes. — What was the *tunica*/tunic?
300: A Roman would have seen this type of competition in the Circus Maximus. — What were chariot races?
400: Gladiatorial shows were held here. — What was the amphitheater/Colosseum?
500: He was the third king of Rome. — Who was Tullius Hostilius?

Round Nine

Grammar

100: This case is used for the object of *vescor.* — What is the ablative?
200: This principal part is used to form the passive voice in the perfect system. — What is the fourth (principal part)?
300: This type of verb is passive in form and active in meaning. — What is a deponent?
400: This verb mood is used in indirect questions. — What is the subjunctive?
500: This part of speech must be in an ablative of manner if *cum* is omitted. — What is an adjective?

Mythology

100: She was the gorgon who gave birth to Pegasus. — Who was Medusa?
200: This creature was the son of the wife of Minos. — Who was the Minotaur?
300: Charon ferries the dead across this river. — What is the Styx?
400: She received the golden apple for the fairest from Paris. — Who was Venus/Aphrodite?
500: He was Ulysses' dog. — Who was Argus?

(cont.)

Vocabulary

100: This is the gender of *pudor*. What is masculine?
200: This is the gender of all Latin nouns ending in the suffix *-men*. What is neuter?
300: This is the genitive plural of *nox*. What is *noctium?*
400: This is the third principal part of *tango*. What is *tetigi?*
500: This Latin word means "a woman's shame or honor" or "modesty." What is *pudor?*

Derivatives

100: This derivative of *nauta* was the name given to Russian spacemen. What is Cosmonaut(s)?
200: This is the Latin noun which gives us a word used in regards to removing a body from a grave. What is *humus?*
300: This Latin noun meaning "host-guest" give us *hospitality*. What is *hospes?*
400: This Latin word for "earth" gives us the name of a heavy earth metal as well as the name of a town in Colorado. What is *tellus?*
500: This Latin noun gives us the heraldic term "escutcheon." What is *scutum?*

History and Life

100: Gaius Julius Caesar was assassinated on the Ides of this month. What is March?
200: This Roman general and dictator defeated Pharnaces. Who was (Gaius Julius) Caesar?
300: The Romans gave this name to the first day of the month. What is *Kalends/Kalendae?*
400: The Roman night was divided into four of these. What are watches?
500: Romulus was given this name after he was deified. What was Quirinus?

Round Ten

Grammar

100: This case follows many verbs compounded with prepositions. What is the dative?
200: *Ecce* and *vae* are this part of speech. What is an interjection?
300: This verb form is used for the verb of an indirect statement What is an infinitive?
400: This verb is used as an auxiliary in forming the passive voice in the perfect system. What is *sum?*
500: *Amatum iri* is this tense of an infinitive. What is future?

Mythology

100: This Herculean task required killing this creature with nine heads. What was the Hydra?
200: The story of this mythological couple is the basis for Shakespeare's *Romeo and Juliet*. Who were Pyramus and Thisbe?
300: She wove the misdeeds of the immortals. Who was Arachne?
400: This was present first, and gives us the word *gas*. What is Chaos?
500: Gods and goddesses had this in their veins. What is *ichor?*

Vocabulary

100: This is the meaning of the adverb *omnino*. What is "in all" or "altogether"?
200: This Latin word means "both." What is *ambo?*
300: This is the gender of *pax*. What is feminine?
400: This is the gender of *morus*, meaning "mulberry tree." What is feminine?
500: This is the fourth principal of *spargo*. What is *sparsus/a/um?*

(cont.)

Derivatives

100: If we give *credence* to something, this is our attitude toward it. What is belief/ we believe it?

200: A hen-pecked husband is described by this derivative from a Latin word for "wife." What is *uxorious?*

300: The Latin verb *curro* gives us this word naming paper money. What is *currency?*

400: This Latin noun gives us *pioneer* and *pawn*. What is *pes?*

500: *Statue* comes from this Latin verb. What is *sto?*

History and Life

100: This king of Rome established the state religion. Who was Numa Pompilius?

200: Her suicide helped to bring about the end of the Monarchy. Who was Lucretia?

300: This person would have worn the *tunica recta*. Who was the bride?

400: Romans almost always diluted this beverage with water. What is wine?

500: This was the Romans' name for the meal we call "lunch." What was *prandium?*

Quaesita Periculo Latino
Advanced Level

Categories are as follow: GRAMMAR, MYTHOLOGY AND LITERATURE, VOCABULARY, DERIVATIVES, and HISTORY AND LIFE.

Round One

GRAMMAR

100: This case is used to show the price. — What is the ablative?
200: This is the principal part upon which the imperfect subjunctive active is formed. — What is the second (principal part)?
300: These Latin words introduce a negative result clause. — What is *ut non?*
400: This Latin word introduces a negative purpose clause. — What is *ne?*
500: This is the case used with *causa* to show purpose. — What is the genitive?

MYTHOLOGY AND LITERATURE

100: He wrote poems about Lesbia. — Who was Catullus?
200: He wrote the *Georgics*. — Who was Vergil?
300: He treasured his Sabine farm. — Who was Horace?
400: She was the mother of the Muses. — Who was Mnemosyne?
500: He was the blind prophet in many tales. — Who was Tiresias?

VOCABULARY

100: This Latin word means "I spare." — What is *parco?*
200: This is the third principal part of *fallo.* — What is *fefelli?*
300: This Latin word means "mindless" or "insane." — What is *amens/demens?*
400: This Latin word means "I smile or laugh at." — What is *rideo?*
500: This is the gender of the names of most trees. — What is feminine?

DERIVATIVES

100: This Latin word gives us *navigational.* — What is *navigo?*
200: Of *flumen, rivus, mare* and *humus,* this word does not belong with the rest because of its meaning. — What is *humus?*
300: This Latin word gives us *cordiality.* — What is *cor?*
400: This Latin noun gives us *fulminate.* — What is *fulmen?*
500: This Latin noun gives us *voluptuous.* — What is *voluptas?*

HISTORY AND LIFE

100: He was the last Julio-Claudian emperor. — Who was Nero?
200: Mark Antony became a bigamist when he married her. — Who was Cleopatra?
300: A relative of Gaius Julius Caesar, he was consul seven times. — Who was Marius?
400: This is the "real" name for the Colosseum. — What is the Flavian Amphitheater?
500: A Thracian gladiator led a slave revolt beginning in this year. — What was 73 B.C.?

Round Two

Grammar

100: This case follows the preposition *coram*. What is the ablative?
200: This is the present imperative singular of *conor*. What is *conare?*
300: This is the perfect active subjunctive, third person plural of *amo*. What is *amaverint?*
400: This is the nominative plural of *mare*. What is *maria?*
500: *Credo* takes its direct object in this case. What is the dative?

Mythology and Literature

100: She is the Goddess of the Hearth for the Romans. Who is Vesta?
200: This couple was visited by Mercury and Jupiter and became trees because they had been hospitable. Who were Baucis and Philemon?
300: Dido commits suicide in this book of the *Aeneid*. What is Book IV?
400: He delivered the *Philippics*. Who was Cicero (or Demosthenes)?
500: He wrote the *Attic Nights* for his children. Who was Aulus Gellius?

Vocabulary

100: This Latin preposition means "like" or "in the image (of)." What is *instar?*
200: This is the third principal part of *parco*. What is *peperci?*
300: This is the gender of *pax*. What is feminine?
400: This word means "death" or "blindness" as well as "night." What is *nox?*
500: This is a Latin word for the absence of *leisure*. What is *negotium?*

Derivatives

100: This derivative lists the places one intends to go to on a journey. What is an *itinerary?*
200: This derivative of *ago* lists things to be done. What is an *agenda?*
300: This Latin noun gives us *auxiliary*. What is *auxilium?*
400: This Latin verb give us *perambulator*. What is *ambulo?*
500: This derivative of *volo, volare* applies to gases. What is *volatile?*

History and Life

100: She was the mother of Romulus and Remus. Who was Rhea Silvia?
200: This Roman king established religion at Rome. Who was Numa Pompilius?
300: The Romans drank this diluted with water. What was wine?
400: This was the toga worn by mourners. What was the *toga pulla?*
500: He was co-consul with Brutus just after the kings were deposed. Who was Collatinus?

Round Three

Grammar

100: This case is used to show duration of time. What is the accusative?
200: This tense of the subjunctive is used for the hortatory. What is the present?
300: This Latin word often appears in the main clause when a *cum* concessive clause is in the sentence. What is *tamen?*
400: This Latin word introduces an optative subjunctive in the imperfect. What is *utinam?*
500: Vergil used this form to show purpose, but Caesar did not. What is an infinitive?

(cont.)

Mythology and Literature

- 100: He wrote the *De Rerum Natura*. — Who was Lucretius?
- 200: There are this many books in the *Aeneid*. — What is twelve?
- 300: She was the mother of Artemis. — Who was Leto?
- 400: She became a nightingale. — Who was Philomela/Philomel?
- 500: Black sails brought his death. — Who was Aegeus?

Vocabulary

- 100: This Latin word means "master" or "lord." — What is *dominus?*
- 200: This Latin word means "master of a ship." — What is *gubernator/magister?*
- 300: This Latin word means, literally, "freeborn children." — What is *liberi?*
- 400: This is the gender of *morus,* a word from Ovid's tale of Pyramus. — What is feminine?
- 500: This is the dative plural of *vis*. — What is *viribus?*

Derivatives

- 100: This Latin verb gives us *malediction*. — What is *dico?*
- 200: This derivative means literally "little shadow." — What is *umbrella?*
- 300: This Latin word is the basis of the name of the Pacific Ocean. — What is *pax/pacifico?*
- 400: This Latin noun gives us *tempestuous*. — What is *tempestas?*
- 500: This derivative refers to a very long word, one "a foot and a half long." — What is *sesquipedalian?*

History and Life

- 100: In ancient times a temple to the god of healing was here; in modern times a hospital is here. — What is Tiber Island?
- 200: Icarus gave his name to this body of water. — What is the Icarian Sea?
- 300: In the form of a bull, Zeus seduced her. — Who was Europa?
- 400: She was the mother of Helen of Troy. — Who is Leda?
- 500: The *pelicula* designated this. — What was a slave's personal property?

Round Four

Grammar

- 100: Verbs of remembering and forgetting are followed by this case. — What is the genitive?
- 200: This is the present imperative plural of *conor*. — What is *conamini?*
- 300: This principal part is the perfect passive participle. — What is the fourth (principal part)?
- 400: This is ablative singular ending for i-stem neuter nouns. — What is "i"?
- 500: The Latin verb *persuadeo* is follow by this case. — What is the dative?

Mythology and Literature

- 100: He was a one-eyed giant whom Odysseus blinded. — Who was Polyphemus?
- 200: He wrote to a historian about the death of his uncle. — Who was Pliny the Younger?
- 300: She was the goddess who cut a lock of Dido's hair. — Who was Iris?
- 400: He wrote letters to his friend "Atticus." — Who was Cicero?
- 500: This work is patterned upon both the *Odyssey* and the *Iliad*. — What is the *Aeneid?*

Vocabulary

- 100: This Latin word is a synonym of *templum*. — What is *fanum/delubrum/aedes/aedicula?*
- 200: This Latin word can mean both "tenement house" and "island." — What is *insula?*
- 300: This is the fourth principal part of *polliceor*. — What is *pollicitus/a/um?*
- 400: This Latin word gives us *onerous*. — What is *onus?*
- 500: This is the Latin word for *business* or *task*. — What is *negotium?*

(cont.)

Derivatives

100: This derivative of *avis* names a man who flies an airplane. What is *aviator?*
200: This derivative of *avis* names a woman who flies an airplane. What is *aviatrix?*
300: This Latin verb is the origin of *influenza.* What is *fluo?*
400: Calculus, a difficult subject, derives its name from this Latin word meaning "little stone." What is *calculus?*
500: This Latin verb gives us *computer* and *count.* What is *puto?*

History and Life

100: He had help from Ariadne in solving a problem. Who was Theseus?
200: He built the labyrinth. Who was Daedalus?
300: They said, "Nos moritur te salutamus." Who were gladiators?
400: Romans were buried outside these. What were the city walls?
500: This is what a Roman might call dessert. What was the *secunda mensa?*

Round Five

Grammar

100: *Coram* takes its object in this case. What is the ablative?
200: This type of verb is passive in form but active in meaning. What is a deponent (verb)?
300: This case is used to show the respect in which something is true. What is the ablative?
400: This is a type of purpose clause introduced by, for example, *qui* or *quae.* What is a relative clause of purpose/relative purpose clause?
500: The jussive subjunctive uses these persons. What are second and third (persons)?

Mythology and Literature

100: Livy's great historical work told the story of the city from its founding. What is *Ab Urbe Condita*?
200: This figure of speech involves the cutting in two of a compound word with another word or other words. What is tmesis?
300: There are this many feet in a pentameter line. What is five?
400: This alone remained in Pandora's box. What is hope?
500: He was chained to a rock for bringing fire to man. Who was Prometheus?

Vocabulary

100: This Latin adverb means "in the meanwhile." What is *interim?*
200: This Latin adverb means "very well." What is *optime?*
300: This is the antonym of *bene.* What is *male?*
400: This is a synonym of *fanum.* What is *templum/aedes/delubrum/aedicula?*
500: This is the third principal part of *tollo.* What is *sustuli?*

Derivatives

100: This Latin adjective gives us *veterinarian.* What is *vetus?*
200: This Latin word gives us *antiquarian.* What is *antiquus/a/um?*
300: This Latin word means "fishlike." What is *piscine?*
400: This is the Latin verb that is the origin of our word *street.* What is *sterno (sternere, stravi, stratum)?*
500: This Latin verb gives us *agile.* What is *ago?*

(cont.)

History and Life

- 100: Gaul as a whole was divided into these many parts. — What are three?
- 200: Of these, a Roman would not have eaten this one: oranges, olives, grapes, cherries. — What are oranges?
- 300: This emperor is sometimes credited with the invention of ice cream because he had snow brought from the Alps and flavored with fruit juice. — Who was Nero?
- 400: A Roman bride's hair was parted with this. — What was a spear/*hasta*?
- 500: A magistrate wore this kind of toga. — What was a *toga praetexta?*

Round Six

Grammar

- 100: This is the present passive infinitive of *duco.* — What is *duci?*
- 200: There is no gerund for this case. — What is the nominative?
- 300: There are these many infinitives in Latin. — What are five (or six)?
- 400: This is the case used to show how long something goes on. — What is the accusative?
- 500: This is the genitive plural of *passus.* — What is *passuum?*

Mythology and Literature

- 100: She is the Greek goddess of love and beauty. — Who is Aphrodite?
- 200: This poet is buried at Naples. — Who was Vergil?
- 300: This poet wrote a moving farewell at his brother's grave. — Who was Catullus?
- 400: She was Dido's late husband's nurse. — Who was Barce?
- 500: This poet ended an epigram with the word *tussit.* — Who was Martial?

Vocabulary

- 100: This Latin deponent verb means "perform." — What is *fungor?*
- 200: This word means "faith." — What is *fides?*
- 300: This is the genitive singular of *res.* — What is *rei?*
- 400: This Latin noun means "life, breath, or soul." — What is *anima?*
- 500: This is the gender of *scriba.* — What is masculine?

Derivatives

- 100: This Latin verb gives us *obsession.* — What is *sedeo/obsideo?*
- 200: This derivative names one who fought with a sword. — What is *gladiator?*
- 300: Ironically, we eat *veal* from a young calf, but its Latin basis means this. — What is old?
- 400: This Latin noun came directly into English to signify a winner. — What is *victor?*
- 500: This adjectival derivative is from the Latin word for crowd. — What is *vulgar?*

History and Life

- 100: A trireme had this many rows of oars. — What is three?
- 200: He was the richest and noblest Helvetian. — Who was Orgetorix?
- 300: A freed slave was called by this Latin word. — What is *libertus?*
- 400: Of the following, a Roman would not have used these: tobacco, beer, whiskey, olive oil. — What are tobacco and whiskey?
- 500: He was the emperor in the East when Romulus Augustulus was overthrown in the West. — Who was Zeno?

Round Seven

Grammar

100: These cases may be used for objects of *potior*. What are ablative and genitive?
200: This is the adverbial superlative of *facile*. What is *facillime?*
300: This is the comparative of *altum*. What is *altius?*
400: This verb form is used in an indirect statement. What is an infinitive?
500: Of these deponent verbs, this one does not take the ablative: *fungor, utor, fruor, hortor*. What is *hortor?*

Mythology and Literature

100: This Greek god had a winged helmet and winged sandals. Who was Hermes?
200: He wrote poem to Lesbia. Who was Catullus?
300: He was the subject of four orations of Cicero, the first of which was given in the senate, the second to the people Who was Catiline?
400: He wrote poems to Delia. Who was Propertius?
500: Aurora had Tithonus turned into a grasshopper because she had forgotten to ask for this. What is perpetual youth?

Vocabulary

100: This Latin idiom means "to wage war." What is *bellum gerere?*
200: This is the antonym of *male*. What is *bene?*
300: This word is out of place in this group: *regina, domina, serva, imperatrix*. What is *serva?*
400: This Latin verb means "lose" or "let go." What is *mitto?*
500: This Latin word means "put out" or "expose." What is *expono?*

Derivatives

100: This deponent verb has *fruit* as one of its derivatives. What is *fruor?*
200: This Latin noun is at the heart of *cordiality*. What is *cor?*
300: This derivative of *navigo* was done first by Magellan's men when they sailed around the world. What is *circumnavigate/circumnavigation?*
400: This Latin noun gives us *obnoxious* and *noisome*. What is *nox?*
500: If you are standing right in the road, you are this derivative. What is *obvious?*

History and Life

100: He got to name the city because he saw twelve birds. Who was Romulus?
200: *Pelicula* belonged to this type of person. What was a slave?
300: A slave was freed by this act. What was *manumission*?
400: This king established Roman religion. Who was Numa (Pompilius)?
500: Rome was founded in this month. What is April?

Round Eight

Grammar

100: Of these prepositions, this one does not take the ablative: *coram, prae, infra, pro*. What is *infra?*
200: This is the third person singular, present subjunctive of *sum*. What is *sit?*
300: This verb mood gives a command. What is the imperative?
400: This is the mood used in an indirect question. What is the subjunctive?
500: Neoptolemus used this verb form to tell Priam to remember to tell his father how bad he had been. What is the future imperative?

(cont.)

Mythology and Literature

100: In the *Iliad* she is called "cow-eyed." — Who is Hera?
200: She is the goddess of the Rainbow and Hera's messenger. — Who is Iris?
300: This oracle gave ambiguous answers. — What was the oracle of Delphi?
400: He wrote the *De Rerum Natura.* — Who was Lucretius?
500: He wrote *Ab Urbe Condita.* — Who was Livy?

Vocabulary

100: This is the meaning of *sum.* — What is "I am'"
200: This Latin in verb is the opposite of *odi.* — What is *amo?*
300: This noun is the opposite of *otium.* — What is *negotium?*
400: This word is out of place in this group: *pono, pons, expono, mitto.* — What is *pons?*
500: This Latin adjective means "very big." — What is *maximus/a/um?*

Derivatives

100: This derivative tells us that a building's stones are falling. — What is *dilapidated*?
200: This is the name of a blue stone, the color of the water of the sea. — What is an *aquamarine?*
300: This Latin verb for cook gave us the Spanish *cocinar.* — What is *coquo?*
400: This Latin verb for think gave us *count.* — What is *puto?*
500: This derivative of *nox* means "foul smelling," and Mark Twain used it in *The Adventures of Huckleberry Finn* when rotten fruit and vegetables were thrown at the King and the Duke. — What is *noisome?*

History and Life

100: This was the site of chariot races. — What was the circus?
200: This was Rome's business and social center. — What was the Forum?
300: This relative of Gaius Julius Caesar was consul seven times. — Who was Marius?
400: Of red, white, blue, green, and brown, this was not a color for a racing faction. — What was brown?
500: This feast was a harvest festival held in December. — What was Saturnalia?

Round Nine

Grammar

100: This degree of adjective or adverb is used with *quam* to show the highest possible degree. — What is the superlative?
200: This case is used for the second term of a comparison when *quam* is not used to mean "than." — What is the ablative?
300: A writer must have one of these in order to use a relative purpose later in the sentence. — What is a direct object?
400: This noun construction explains or identifies another noun. — What is an appositive?
500: *Patre sublato* is this kind of construction. — What is an ablative absolute?

Mythology and Literature

100: This figure of speech has a pattern of "ABBA." — What is chiasmus?
200: *Velut* introduces this figure of speech — What is a simile?
300: He is king of the gods and father of men in the *Aeneid.* — Who is Jupiter?
400: He is the Greek god of love. — Who is Eros?
500: He had an oracle at Dodona, whose prophecies were interpreted by the rustling of oak leaves. — Who was Zeus?

(cont.)

Vocabulary

- 100: This Latin noun means "delay." What is *mora?*
- 200: This Latin verb means "I die." What is *morior?*
- 300: This is the gender of *vulgus.* What is neuter?
- 400: This is the second principal part of *tollo.* What is *tollere?*
- 500: This is the Latin antonym of *amo.* What is *odi?*

Derivatives

- 100: This derivative naming a part of the body means literally "little mouse." What is muscle?
- 200: This derivative means "like a cat." What is feline?
- 300: This Latin noun gives us *manufacture.* What is *manus?*
- 400: A *moratorium* occurs when we do this. What is delay?
- 500: *Luxury* is not derived from this Latin noun, but *lucency* is. What is *lux?*

History and Life

- 100: This Latin phrase was used like our phrase "from soup to nuts." What is *"ab ovo usque ad mala"*?
- 200: This person called out names for his patron. What was the *nomenclator?*
- 300: He was a Carthaginian general who led elephants across the Alps. Who was Hannibal?
- 400: There were these many Punic Wars. What are three?
- 500: Oadacer became King of Rome in this year. What was A.D. 476?

Round Ten

Grammar

- 100: There are these many declensions of nouns. What are five?
- 200: This declension has a sub-class called i-stem. What is the third declension?
- 300: If the first term of a comparison is in the nominative, and *quam* is used to mean "than," the second term of the comparison is in this case. What is the nominative?
- 400: This case is used for a predicate adjective when the form of *sum* used is *esse.* What is the accusative?
- 500: *Sunto* is in this tense. What is the future?

Mythology and Literature

- 100: He was known as Rome's greatest orator. Who was Cicero?
- 200: She was the sister and wife of Jupiter. Who was Juno?
- 300: She ate six seeds and so had to remain where she was for six months every year. Who was Persephone/Proserpina?
- 400: He was the author of *Attic Nights.* Who was Aulus Gellius?
- 500: He wrote about a city mouse and a country mouse. Who was Horace?

Vocabulary

- 100: This Latin idiom means "to form a plan." What is *consilium capere?*
- 200: This is the meaning of *bellum gerere* in English. What is "to wage war"?
- 300: This is the gender of *aequor* and *mare.* What is neuter?
- 400: This is the third principal part of *parco.* What is *peperci?*
- 500: This is the gender of *pax.* What is feminine?

(cont.)

Derivatives

100:	This Latin noun gives us the word *umbrella* and means also *ghost*.	What is *umbra?*
200:	This Latin adverb gives us the Spanish word *manana*.	What is *mane?*
300:	This Latin noun gives us *muscle*.	What is *mus?*
400:	This derivative lists things to be done.	What is an *agenda?*
500:	This Latin noun gives us the word *pace*.	What is *passus?*

History and Life

100:	The Colosseum was completed in this year.	What was (A.D.) 80?
200:	This dynasty followed the Julio-Claudians.	What was the Flavian Dynasty?
300:	He was the last Julio-Claudian emperor.	Who was Nero?
400:	The Romans used this substance the way we use butter.	What was olive oil?
500:	He was co-consul with Collatinus.	Who was Brutus?

Fifty General Knowledge Questions for Periculum Latinum

1. This is the motto of the United States.
   What is "e pluribus unum"?
2. This abbreviation means "that is" or "it is."
   What is i.e.?
3. This abbreviation means "for example."
   What is e.g.?
4. This is the Latin phrase for "time flies."
   What is "tempus fugit"?
5. This is the English meaning of the abbreviation Q.E.D.
   What is "that which had/has to be shown"?
6. This is the genitive of *hic*.
   What is huius?
7. This is the genitive of *is*.
   What is eius?
8. This Latin demonstrative means "that of yours."
   What is iste?
9. This Latin phrase means "at that time."
   What is illo tempore?
10. This is the neuter of *ille*.
    What is illud?
11. This is the motto of Virginia.
    What is "Sic semper tyrannis"?
12. This is the Latin for the abbreviation Q.E.D.
    What is "Quod erat/est demonstrandum"?
13. This Latin phrase, found on the back of a dollar bill, means "He (God) has favored our beginnings."
    What is "Annuit coeptis"?
14. This motto means "to the stars through difficulties."
    What is "Ad astra per aspera"?
15. This motto means "out of many, one."
    What is "e pluribus unum"?
16. This temple was built in Rome to all the gods.
    What was the Pantheon?
17. This was the wall down the middle of the Circus Maximus.
    What was the spina?
18. This was the starting gate in a circus.
    What was the carcer?
19. These were the four main colors of racing factions.
    What were red, white, blue, and green?
20. The Colosseum was once flooded for this.
    What was a naumachia/mock naval battle?

(cont.)

21. This site in Athens was comparable to the Forum in Rome.
What was the agora?

22. The Parthenon was built on top of this.
What was the Acropolis?

23. He was the great lawgiver of Athens.
Who was Solon?

24. This island was the site of the labyrinth.
What was Crete?

25. This Greek philosopher, condemned to drink hemlock for corrupting the morals of youth, had been a shoemaker.
Who was Socrates?

26. This emperor built a wall between what are today England and Scotland.
Who was Hadrian?

27. This woman was the queen of the Iceni, a British tribe.
Who was Boudica/Boadicea?

28. The Roman name for this English town was *Aquae Sulis.*
What is Bath?

29. If an English town had been a Roman camp, its modern name ends in one of these: -chester, -orum, -ton, -don.
What is -chester?

30. This is the Latin for "New Scotland."
What is Nova Scotia?

31. This was the Roman name for their province which we now call Spain.
What was Hispania?

32. This was the Roman name for their province which we now call Romania.
What was Dacia?

33. This was the Roman name for France.
What was Gallia?

34. This was the Roman name for Ireland.
What was Hibernia?

35. This was the Roman name for Paris, France.
What was Lutetia?

36. This case is used to show extent of space.
What is the accusative?

37. *Amavero* is in this tense.
What is the future perfect?

38. A gerundive is used as this part of speech.
What is an adjective?

39. This construction, used with a dative of agent, shows necessity or obligation.
What is the passive periphrastic/the second periphrastic?

40. This form is used in place of the nominative case for a gerund.
What is the (present) infinitive/second principal part?

41. This case may be used with some form of *sum* to show possession.
What is the dative?

42. This voice shows that the subject is acted upon by an agent.
What is the passive (voice)?

(cont.)

43. These letters are the tense indicator for the imperfect.
What are "b" and "a"/"ba"?

44. This emperor was supposedly poisoned by mushrooms.
Who was Claudius?

45. Rome is located on this river.
What is the Tiber?

46. There are these many islands in the Tiber.
What is one?

47. He boasted that he found Rome a city of brick and left it a city of marble.
Who was Augustus?

48. He was the dictator who forced Caesar to divorce Cornelia.
Who was Sulla?

49. These many men formulated the Laws of the Twelve Tables.
What were ten?

50. She was the mother of Caesarion.
Who was Cleopatra?

Chapter Six

Nix, Mox, Mons and Mens Driving Kids Out of Their Minds

The following lists contain words commonly confused. The lists are divided by levels at which they may be used. Teach the words a few at a time, as I have them grouped. The following guidelines describe a successful sequence for teaching these words.

1. Put the words in each group onto the chalkboard or a transparency for the overhead projector. You may photocopy these pages and make transparencies of them. On the overhead simply cover with a piece of paper the groups not being taught.

2. Pronounce the words and have the students repeat the correct pronunciation after you.

3. Discuss English words that are derived from each Latin word or have the students find the derivatives themselves, using an English dictionary. If you choose to have the students find the derivatives themselves, you might consider doing this in a cooperative learning approach. You might also consider having the students illustrate the Latin words and derivatives via the drawing of derivative trees or the making of collages or mobiles. Discussing or finding derivatives for each Latin word will help the students to remember the meanings.

4. Give a quiz the second or third class day after introducing the words. It is helpful if the students, in preparing for the quiz, make a Latin sentence using each word correctly.

5. After several group of words have been taught and quizzed, prepare a review session. This is a good place to use a classroom game. The words, their meanings, and their derivatives may be reviewed in a *Jeopardy* or *Certamen* format; in a *Win, Lose, or Draw* format; or in many other game formats.

N.B. For various reasons and purposes, some words will appear in more than one group and at more than one level.

Latin One Confusing Words

Group A

via, viae, f.—road, street, way
vīlla, vīllae, f.—farmhouse
vīs, f.—force
vir, virī, m.—man, husband, hero
vērus, vēra, vērum—true

Group B

mōs, mōris, m.—custum
mox—soon
nox, noctis, f.—night
nix, nivis, f.—snow
nex, necis, f.—death

Group C

ab—from, away from, by
ad—to, toward, near, next to, against
at—but
et—and, also, even
est—he, she, or it is

Group D

puella, puellae, f.—girl
puer, puerī, m.—boy
fīlia, fīliae, f.—daughter
fīlius, fīlī, m.—son
fēmina, fēminae, m.—woman

Group E

puella, puellae, f.—girl
pulcher, pulchra, pulchrum—pretty, beautiful, fine
īnsula, īnsulae, f.—island, block, tenement house
incola, incolae, c.—inhabitant
incolō, incolere, incoluī, ___—live in, inhabit, dwell

Group F

ē/ex—from, out of
et—and
edō, ēsse, ēdī, ēsum—eat
ēdō, edere, ēdidī, ēditus—give out
do, dāre, dedī, datum—give
duo, duae, duo—two

Latin Two Confusing Words

Group A

rēx, rēgis, m.—king
rēgīna, rēgīnae, f.—queen
regō, regere, rēxī, rēctum—rule
regnō, regnāre, regnāvī, regnātum—rule
regiō, regiōnis, f.—region
rēgius, rēgia, rēgium—royal
rēgia, rēgiae, f.—palace
rēgnum, rēgnī, n.—kingdom, royal power

Group B

mōns, montis, m.—mountain
mens, mentis, f.—mind
mors, mortis, f.—death
mora, morae, f.—delay
morior, morī, mortuus sum—die
moror, morāri, morātum sum—delay
mortālis, mortāle—mortal
mōs, mōris, m.—custom

Group C

negō, negāre, negāvī, negātum—say no, deny
necō, necāre, necāvī, necātum—kill
nex, necis, f.—death
noceō, nocēre, nocuī, nocitum—harm
nox, noctis, f.—night, death, blindness, moral blindness

Group D

cadō, cadere, cecidī, cāsum—fall
caedō, caedere, cecīdī, caesum—cut down, fell, kill
cāsus, cāsūs, m.—casualty, downfall
casa, casae, f.—house, cottage
causa, causae, f.—cause, case
cauda, caudae, f.—tail

Group E

mēns, mentis, f.—mind
āmens, āmentis—insane
dēmens, dēmentis—insane
amans, amantis—loving
mensa, mensae, f.—table
mensis, mensis, m.—month

Group F

lac, lactis, n.—milk
lacus, lacūs, m.—lake
lex, lēgis, f.—law
lateō, latēre, latuī, ___—hide, lie hidden
*pateō, patēre, patuī,*___—be open
aper, aprī, m.—wild boar
aperiō, aperīre, aperuī, apertum—open
āter, ātra, ātrum—flat black
niger, nigra, nigrum—shiny black

Advanced Latin Confusing Words

Group A

mōs, mōris, m.—custom
mors, mortis, f.—death
moror, morāri, moratus sum—delay
mōrus, mōrī, f.—mulberry tree
dolus, dolī, m.—trick
dolor, dolōris, m.—grief, pain, sorrow
dōnō, dōnāre, dōnāvī, dōnātum—give

Group B

ōs, ōris, n.—mouth
(pl.: face, by synecdoche)
ōra, ōrae, f.—seashore
os, ossis, m.—bone
hōra, hōrae, f.—hour
ōrō, ōrāre, ōrāvī, ōrātum—pray, beg for
ōrnō, ōrnāre, ōrnāvī, ōrnātum—decorate, adorn
honor, honōris, m.—honor

Group C

ferō, ferre, tulī, lātum—bring, bear, carry
ferio, ferīre, ____, _____—strike
fēriae, fēriārum, f. pl.—holidays, vacation, leisure
ferrum, ferrī, n.—iron
(sword, by metonymy)
forum, forī, n.—forum
fax, facis, f.—torch
facio, facere, fēcī, factum—make, do
faciēs, faciēi, f.—face

Group D

vulgus, vulgī, m.—crowd, mob, common people
vultus, vultūs, m.—face, expression, countenance
volucris, volucris, f.—bird, vulture
volō, volāre, volāvī, volātum—fly, rush
volō, velle, voluī, ___—wish, want
mālō, mālle, maluī, ___—prefer
vōx, vōcis, f.—voice, word
vocō, vocāre, vocāvī, vocātum—call

Group E

multus, multa, multum—much
multī, multae, multa—many
parvus, parva, parvum—small
paucī, paucae, pauca—few
paulum—a little, to some extent
paulus, paula, paulum—small, insignificant

Group F

pār, paris—equal
pariēs, pariētis, f.—walls of a house
pars, partis, f.—part
moenia, moeniōrum, n. pl.—wall of a city
(city, by synecdoche)
moneō, monēre, monuī, monitum—warn, advise
mordeō, mordēre, morsī, morsum—bite
maneō, manēre, mānsī, mānsum/mānsūrus—remain, stay
manus, manūs, f.—hand

Group G

amō, amāre, amāvī, amātum—love, like
amans, amantis—loving, lover
āmens, āmentis—insane
dēmens, dēmentis—insane
autem—moreover
tamen—nevertheless, however
tandem—finally
nōmen, nōminis, n.—name
nūmen, nūminis, n.—godhead
flūmen, flūminis, n.—river
fulmen, fulminis, n.—thunderbolt
sumus—we are
summus, summa, summum—top of
nummus, nummī, m.—coin

An Auxiliary List of Confusing Words

A through B

ācer, ācris, ācre—fierce, sharp
ācriter—boldly
aequus, aequa, aequum—fair, equal, just
āēr, āeris, m.—air
aestās, aestātis, f.—summer
aestus, aestūs, m.—tide
aetās, aetātis, f.—age
ager, agrī, m.—field
agō, agere, ēgī, āctum—do, drive
ala, alae, f.—wing
alō, alere, aluī, alitum—feed, nourish
āra, ārae, f.—altar
arca, arcae, f.—box, chest
arceō, arcēre, arcuī, ___—shut out, keep out
arcus, arcūs, m.—bow, rainbow, curve
ardeō, ardēre, ārsī, ārsum—burn, be eager
arō, arāre, arāvī, arātum—plow
audācter—boldy
audāx, audācis—bold, daring
audeō, audēre, ausus sum—dare
audiō, audīre, audīvī, audītum—hear, listen to
aura, aurae, f.—breeze, air
aureus, aurea, aureum—golden, of gold
auris, auris, f.—ear
aurum, aurī, n.—gold
ausus, ausī, n.—daring deed or act

C through D

cēdō, cēdere, cessī, cessum—yield
coma, comae, f.—hair, foliage
comes, comitis, c.—companion
crēdō, crēdere, crēdidī, crēditum—believe, trust
*discō, discere, didicī,*___—learn
doceō, docēre, docuī, doctum—teach
doleō, dolēre, doluī, dolitum—grieve
dolor, dolōris, m.—pain, grief, sorrow
dolus, dolī, m.—trick
dominus, dominī, m.—master, lord
domus, domūs, f.—home
dōnum, dōnī, n.—gift

E through J

erat—he/she/it was
errat—he/she/it wanders
errō, errāre, errāvī, errātum—wander, stray
erō—I shall be
gena, genae, f.—cheek
genitor, genitōris, m.—father
genetrix, genetrīcis, f.—mother
gēns, gentis, f.—tribe
genū, genūs, n.—knee
genus, generis, m.—type, kind
inter—between, among
intra—within
iūs, iūris, n.—law
iūs, iūris, n.—soup
iussus, iussūs, m.—order

L through M

lābor, lābī, lapsus sum—slip
labor, labōris, m.—work, labor
labōrō, labōrāre, labōrāvī, labōrātum—work
laetus, laeta, laetum—happy, joyful, glad
lātus, lāta, lātum—wide
latus, lateris, n.—side, flank
lectus, lectī, m.—couch
legō, legere, lēgī, lēctum—read
lēx, lēgis, f.—law
liber, librī, m.—book
līber, lībera, līberum— free
līberī, -ōrum, m. pl.—children
līmen, liminis, n.—threshold
lūmen, luminis, n.—light, eye
lūx, lūcis, f.—light

magnus, magna, magnum—great, large
magus, magī, m.—wise man, magician
māla, mālae, f.—jaw
malō, mālle, maluī, ___—prefer
mālum, malī, n.—apple
mālus, malī, m.—mast of a ship
malus, mala, malum—bad
mel, mellis, n.—honey
mīles, mīlitis, m.—soldier
mīlle—one thousand

N through P

nanciscor, nanciscī, nactus sum—to get by accident, to obtain
nāscor, nascī, nātus sum—be born
nātus, nātī, m.—son
novus, nova, novum—new, strange
nurus, nurūs, f.—daughter-in-law
nūtrix, nūtricis, f.—nurse
pānis, pānis, m.—bread
pār, paris—equal
parvus, parva, parvum—small
passer, passeris, m.—sparrow
passus, passa, passum—having suffered
passus, passūs, m.—pace
patior, patī passum sum—suffer
paucī, paucae, pauca—few
per—through
potior, potīrī, potītus sum—gain possession of

Q through Z

sāl, sālis, m.—salt
salūs, salūtis, f.—safety
sedeō, sedēre, sedī, sessum—sit
sēdēs, sēdis, f.—seat, location, chair
sīdus, sīderis, n.—star
sōl, sōlis, m.—sun
solium, soliī, n.—seat, throne, dominion, bathtub
solum, solī, n.—ground, soil
sōlus, sōla, sōlum—only, alone
vīctus, vīctus, m.—food, victuals, livelihood, way of living
videō, vidēre, vīdī, vīsum—see
vinciō, vincīre, vinxī, vinctum—chain, bind
vincō, vincere, vīcī, victum—conquer, win
vir, virī, m.—man
vīs, vīs, f.—strength, *pl. vires, virium*
vulgus, vulgī, n.—crowd
vultus, vultūs, m.—face, facial expression

Ad Astra Per Aspera

Chapter Seven

Making the Aeneid a Matter for Focused Reading

Each year at the beginning of the year, I assign each of my Advanced Placement Vergil students at least one specialty for the *Aeneid*. If the class is small, I assign each student two or three. The students are to notice their specialties as they read and to point out their occurrences to the other members of the class. They explain how the occurrence fits into the whole epic and any symbolism connected to the specialty. They also note recurrences. When they come to the final examination, they bring with them an essay on one of their specialties, and the essay counts 25% of the grade on the final examination. I find that assigning the topics focuses the students' reading and helps them to appreciate the *Aeneid* more. A list of these specialties is on the next page, ready for you to photocopy if you choose.

In addition to noting and discussing these specialties, my students and I discuss the many themes which are present in the *Aeneid*. There are many themes in Vergil's epic, but my students and I have identified eight major themes which yield good classroom discussion and a greater understanding of Vergil's work. For your convenience a list is included in this chapter.

Students also need to practice and learn the figures of speech. I have also found it helpful to discuss with the students what a particular figure of speech contributes to the lines, sentence, paragraph, *etc.* For example, tmesis or anastrophe often occurs when the speaker is confused, agitated, or disturbed as when Dido says, "*Sed mihi vel Tellus optem prius ima dehiscat / vel pater omnipotens adigat me fulmine ad umbras... / ante, pudor quam te violo....*" (But I wish the earth would gape open to me before or the father all powerful would drive me to the shades...before I violate [you], Chastity, or break [your] laws.—Tr. Gaylan Dubose.) Other times the arrangement of words may form a picture of the idea. In Book IV, lines 165–166, for example, the chiasmus found in "*Speluncam Dido dux et Troianus eandem devenient....*" actually places Dido and Aeneas in the same cave. A sample list of figures of speech along with an answer key is contained in this chapter. You may require only one figure to be identified when there are more than one per item. You may also choose to put a "figures bank" on the board or overhead projector. I find it helps to do so; however, I do not include a bank on the tests. An alphabetized list of the figures is included in the answer key in this chapter.

By incorporating the techniques above into the reading of the *Aeneid*, both the lines required by the Advanced Placement syllabus and the entire *Aeneid* in English translation, I have found that my students' scores on the A.P. Vergil Examination have improved. I hope that the following pages are useful to you and your students.

Specialties for the Aeneid

1. flame, fire, burning (II.298–335, II. 681–686)
2. birds (I.393–400, VI.190–192)
3. clouds (I.88–91, IV. 120–123)
4. wind (I.81–86, I. 132–141)
5. food and meals (I.208–222, VII.107–116)
6. gold, silver, and bronze (IV.137–139, VI.671–674)
7. the numbers 3, 4, and 7 (I.187–193, II.692–794)
8. snakes (II.200–227, II.469–475)
9. dreams and apparitions (II.268–295, II.767–794)
10. analogues of fire: lust, passion, heat, possibly light, stars (IV.1–2, IV.300–303)
11. disguises (I.314–320, I.689–694)
12. sacrifices (II.130–144, VI.37–39)
13. relationships between parents and children (I.254–295, I.387–392)
14. portents, omens, and warnings (II.40–55, III.535–547)
15. offerings (IV.504–521, VI.77–83)
16. prophecies (I.261–296, VI.846–853)
17. sports (V.362–484, V.545–603)
18. trees and the cutting of trees (I.175, IV.441–446)
19. embroidery and textiles (I.647–652, I.700)
20. light (I.142–147, IV.584–585)
21. darkness (I.89, VI.450–451)
22. prayer (II.206–218, VI.56–76)
23. walls (II.234–235, VIII.714–716)
24. ships (I.103–123; V.641–663, 685–699)
25. animals (II.469–473, IV.365–367)

These citations are by no means exhaustive, nor are they meant to be. I believe your students will be interested to see that many of the specialities overlap. For example, when Venus appears to Aeneas disguised as a huntress in Book I, she is most definitely his mother, yet she is still very much the goddess.

Themes in the Aeneid

1. The great difficulty in founding a nation. (I.1–11, I.29–33, VII.206–12)

2. The working of fate. (I.1–2, VI.882–886)

3. The importance of piety, honor, and duty. (I.8–11, VI.142–151, VI.847–853)

4. The importance of personal courage. (XII.928–951)

5. The relationships of gods and goddesses to human beings (on all levels). (I.36–49, IV.259–282, IV.693–705, VII.341–358)

6. The importance of submitting the individual will to benefit the state; i.e., civilization. (IV.356–361, XII.928–951)

7. The death of the good and the young in battle. (IX.402–545, XI.818–831, XII.950–951)

8. The relationships of light and dark, calm and storm, good and evil, peace and war, prosperity and trouble ("Just when you thought it was safe...." But look at the end: Aeneas wins. Rome does become great.) (I.34–38, VII.15–45, VIII.106–134)

Definitions and Examples of Some Major Figures of Speech

I have found that it helps to give students examples in English when first defining figures of speech for them. Most of the English examples below I made up. Your students might have fun making up some of their own or finding examples in literature, especially British literature.

alliteration: the repetition of initial consonant sounds
Examples: Sally sells sea shell down by the seashore; *qui tela Typhoia temnis* (I.665)

anaphora: the repetition of words in the beginning of phrases, clauses, or lines
Examples: I shall not listen, I shall not understand, I shall not forgive; *saevus ubi Aeacidae telo iacet Hector, ubi ingens/Sarpedon, ubi tot Simois* . . . (I.99–100)

anastrophe: a reversal of usual word order
Examples: I wound the rope the post around; *maria omnia circum* (I.32)

aposiopesis: a sudden breaking off
Examples: I'm going to . . .; *quos ego* . . . (I.135)

apostrophe: addressing someone who is absent as present or something inanimate as animate
Examples: O stars, gleam for me; *Priamque arx alta, maneres* (II.56)

chiasmus: word order setting up the pattern of ABBA, often used as a framing technique
Examples: Truth is beauty, beauty truth; *speluncam Dido dux et Troianus eandem/ deveniunt* (IV.165–166)

metonymy: the use of something closely associated with a thing to mean the thing itself
Examples: The red baseball cap walked in the door; *Arma virumque cano* (I.1)

onomatopoeia: the use of words whose sounds suggest their meanings, sound symbolism
Examples: Snap, Crackle and Pop; *cum Iuno, aeternum servans sub pectore vulnus* (I.36)

polysyndeton: the use of many conjunctions, usually in the *Aeneid* illustrated with *-que…-que*
Examples: I ran up and he was hurt and I started giving CPR and…, *Insequitur clamorque virum stridorque rudentum* (I.87)

simile: a comparison using *like* or *as*
Examples: Her legs were like toothpicks; *Atque veluti magna in populo cum saepe coorta est….* (I.148ff.) [Latin words introducing similes are *similis, qualis, ut, velut, veluti, sicut, ceu, non aliter quam*]

synchysis: word order setting up the pattern of ABAB, sometimes called interlocking word order
Examples: mine red, his blue, *fortemque Gyan, fortemque Cloanthum* (I.222)

synechdoche: the use of the part to represent the whole; or, according to some, also the use of the whole for the part
Examples: I need to get some wheels; *os umerosque deo similis* (I.589)

Figures of Speech
Advanced Placement—Vergil

Identify the figures of speech found in the items below. Some items may contain more than one figure, and underlined words are clues.

1. Arma virumque canō...

2. Ō terque quarterque beātī...

3. ...magnō miscērī murmure pontum...

4. Quōs ego—sed mōtōs praestat compōnere fluctūs.

5. bis medium amplexī, bis collo squāmea...

6. ...Pyrrhus
   exsultat, tēlīs et lūce coruscus aēna;
   quālis ubī in lūcem coluber...

7. Tum pavidae tēctīs mātrēs ingentibus errant...

8. Spēluncam Dīdō dux et Trōiānus eandem dēveniunt...

9. tot vigilēs oculī subter, mīrābile dictū,
   tot linguae, totidem ōra sonant, tot surrigit aurēs.

10. ...circum terga datī...

11. ...validīs ingentem viribus hastam...

12. ...Priamīque arx alta, manērēs.

13. Bis cōnātus erat cāsūs effingere in aurō;
    bis patriae cecidere manūs.

14. unde ruunt totidem vōcēs, respōnsa Sibyllae.

15. ...ac ventī, velut agmine factō,
    ...ruunt et terrās turbine perflant.

(cont.)

Perīculum Latīnum

Grammar	Myth/Lit	Vocabulary	Derivatives	History/Life
100	100	100	100	100
200	200	200	200	200
300	300	300	300	300
400	400	400	400	400
500	500	500	500	500

Advanced

16. Tū mihi, quodcumque hoc rēgnī, tū scēptra Iovemque
conciliās, tū dās epulīs accumbere divum...

17. ...revocāte animōs, maestumque timōrem mittite...

18. amissōs longō sociōs sermōne requirunt...

19. ...Et sī fāta deum, sī mēns nōn laeva fuisset...

20. Mūsa, mihī causās memorā...

21. Tum Cererem corruptam undīs Cerealiāque arma expediunt fessī rērum...

22. ante, Pudor, quam...

23. nec prius abstitit quam septem ingentia vicora corpora fundat humī...

24. panduntur portae; iuvat īre et Dōrica castra
dēsertōsque vidēre locōs litusque relictum.

25. Ītaliam contrā

Key for Practice on Figures of Speech

You may require only one figure to be identified when there is more than one per item. You may choose to put a "figures bank" on the board or overhead projector. I find it helps to do so; however, I do not put a bank up when I test. An alphabetized list of the figures involved in this practice follows at the end of the key. (Be sure to follow up the practice of identifying with a discussion of the effect of the figure; *e.g.*, tmesis or anastrophe often occurs when the speaker is confused, agitated, or disturbed. Pay especial attention to item number 8: Who is the leader? Note how the chiasmus actually puts Dido and Aeneas inside the same cave.)

1.	metonymy	(Book I.1)
2.	polysyndeton	(Book I.94–95)
3.	alliteration	(Book I.124)
4.	aposiopesis	(Book I.135)
5.	anaphora	(Book II.218)
6.	simile	(Book II.469–470)
7.	synchysis	(Book II.489)
8.	chiasmus, alliteration	(Book IV.165–166)
9.	anaphora	(Book IV.182–183)
10.	tmesis	(Book II.218–219)
11.	synchysis	(Book II.50)
12.	apostrophe	(Book II.56)
13.	anaphora, alliteration	(Book VI.32–33)
14.	onomatopoeia	(Book VI.44)
15.	simile	(Book I.82–83)
16.	anaphora	(Book I.78–79)
17.	synchysis	(Book I.202–203)
18.	synchysis	(Book I.217)
19.	anaphora	(Book II.54)
20.	alliteration	(Book I.8)
21.	metonymy	(Book I.177)
22.	tmesis	(Book IV.27)
23.	tmesis	(Book I.192)
24.	alliteration	(Book II.27–28)
25.	anastrophe	(Book I.13)

Figure Bank

alliteration	**aposiopesis**	**metonymy**	**simile**
anaphora	**apostrophe**	**onomatopoeia**	**synchysis**
anastrophe	**chiasmus**	**polysyndeton**	**tmesis**

Chapter Eight
Certamina

Most students love "to play" certamen. Naturally, a teacher will not want to use the game every day or even every week; however, once or twice a month works out well. I use either questions I have already or compose new questions focussing upon recent lessons. The use of certamen is an excellent way to review for major tests, especially for the Advanced Placement class.

Since a maximum of twelve students can play at a time, I announce at the beginning that I may call on anyone in the room at any time for an answer. This practice ensures that all students—ideally—must listen.

As you review the questions for certamen in this book, you may occasionally find repeats. I do not think these repeats are bad, since I feel that anything can be a learning tool; and, if a student learns from one round to another or even in the same round, so much the better.

I hope you will find these rounds useful and helpful to your students.

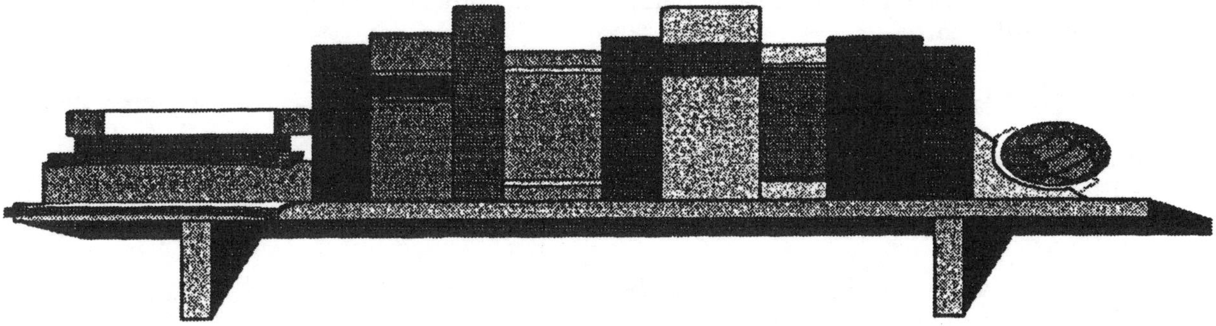

Novice Certamen

Round I

1. Give the fourth principal part of *do*. **datus/datum**
   - B1: Give the fourth principal part of *sum*. **futurus/futurum**
   - B2: Give the fourth principal part of *iuvo*. **iutus/iutum**

2. Give the Latin noun and its English meaning from which we derive *amity*. **amicitia (friendship)**
   - B1: Give the Latin noun and its English meaning from which we derive *nuministic*. **numen (divine spirit, nod, divinity)**
   - B2: Give the Latin noun and its English meaning from which we derive *liberty*. **libertas (freedom)**

3. Who was the king of Troy during the Trojan War? **Priam**
   - B1: Who was his queen? **Hecuba**
   - B2: Who was their son-in-law, the husband of Creusa? **Aeneas**

4. Say in Latin "out of many, one." **e pluribus unum**
   - B1: Say in Latin "that is." **id est**
   - B2: Say in Latin "for example." **exempli gratia**

5. Say in Latin "Many girls were shouting." **Multae puellae clamabant.**
   - B1: Make *clamabant* future. **clamabunt**
   - B1: Change *clamabunt* to the perfect. **clamaverunt**

6. Complete this analogy: Ulysses is to Penelope as Hector is to _________. **Andromache**
   - B1: Prometheus is to Epimetheus as Castor is to _________. **Pollux**
   - B2: Castor is to Pollux as Romulus is to _________. **Remus**

7. Who succeeded Augustus as emperor? **Tiberius**
   - B1: On what island did Tiberius spend his last years? **Capri**
   - B2: Which emperor is reported to have fiddled while Rome burned? **Nero**

8. Which word does not have the same Latin root as the others: adhere, adhesive, exhaust, adherent? **exhaust**
   - B1: What Latin verb is common to the other three words? **haereo**
   - B2: What Latin verb gives us *exhaust*? **haurio**

9. Which was the first of the Roman hills to be settled? **the Palatine**
   - B1: Give the month, day, and year of the founding or Rome. **April 21, 753 B.C.**
   - B2: How did Remus die? **Romulus killed him.**

10. What name is given to the series of wars between Rome and Carthage? **the Punic Wars**
    - B2: How many Punic Wars were there? **three**
    - B3: What queen had founded Carthage? **Dido/Elissa**

11. Who was the second king of Rome? **Numa Pompilius**
    - B1: Who was the fifth king of Rome? **Tarquinius Priscus**
    - B2: Who was the last king of Rome? **Tarquinius Superbus**

(cont.)

12. Who was the great-uncle and adoptive father of Octavian? **(Gaius Julius) Caesar**
- B1: Who was G. Julius Caesar's last wife? **Calpurnia**
- B2: What title was added to Octavian's name after he became emperor? **Augustus**

13. For the verb *amo*, give the third person singular, passive voice. **amatur**
- B1: Change *amatur* to second person. **amaris**
- B2: Make *amaris* plural. **amamini**

14. Which word does not belong with the others because of its meaning: *nauta, poeta, manus, agricola*? **manus**
- B1: What is the meaning of *manus*? **hand**
- B2: What is unusual about the other three words? **They are masculine of the first declension.**

15. What word does not belong with the others because of its gender: *amicus, incola, corpus, gladius*? **corpus**
- B1: What gender is *corpus*? **neuter**
- B2: What gender are the other three? **masculine**

16. For the noun *flumen* give the accusative plural. **flumina**
- B1: Define *flumen*. **river, stream**
- B2: Define *fluo*. **flow**

17. What would a Roman have done in the *culina*? **cooked**
- B1: In what room would a Roman have slept? **cubiculum**
- B2: In what room was the *impluvium*? **atrium**

18. Who was the Greek goddess of agriculture and grain? **Demeter**
- B1: Who was her daughter? **Persephone**
- B2: What is Demeter's Roman name? **Ceres**

19. What case follows the preposition *circum*? **accusative**
- B1: What case follows the preposition *ex*? **ablative**
- B2: What case follows the preposition *inter*? **accusative**

20. What was the name given to the gods of the pantry? **penates**
- B1: Who was the *paterfamilias*? **the father**
- B2: Who was a *filius*? **a son**

Novice Certamen
Round II

1. Give the third principal part of *sto*. **steti**
   - B1: Give the third principal part of *sum*. **fui**
   - B2: Give the third principal part of *eo*. **ii OR ivi**

2. Give the Latin noun and its English meaning from which we derive *incorporeal*. **corpus (body)**
   - B1: Give the Latin noun and its English meaning from which we derive *lucency*. **lux (light)**
   - B2: Give the Latin noun and its English meaning from which we derive *vermiform*. **vermis (worm) OR forma (shape)**

3. How long did the war between Greece and Troy last? **ten years**
   - B1: How long did Aeneas wander before arriving at Carthage? **seven years**
   - B2: How long did Ulysses wander before arriving at Ithaca? **ten years**

4. Say in Latin, "for the time being." **pro tempore**
   - B1: Say in Latin, "Time flies." **Tempus fugit.**
   - B2: Say in Latin, "The time is at hand." **Tempus adest.**

5. Define *lex*. **law**
   - B1: Define *rex*. **king**
   - B2: Define *nox*. **night, death, blindness, moral blindness, darkness**

6. Say in Latin, "Many sailors sailed." **Multi nautae navigabant. OR Multi nautae navigaverunt.**
   - B1: Say in Latin, "No poets wrote well." **Nulli poetae bene scribebant. OR Nulli poetae bene scripserunt.**
   - B2: Say in Latin "My mother was sitting." **Mea mater sedebat.**

7. Complete this analogy: Adam:Eve::______:Pandora. **Epimetheus**
   - B1: Eve:Pandora::Samson:______. **Hercules**
   - B2: Samson:Absolom::Hercules:______. **Adonis**

8. Who was the last emperor of the Julio-Claudian dynasty? **Nero**
   - B1: Who was the first emperor of the Julio-Claudian dynasty? **Augustus**
   - B2: Who was the successor of Augustus? **Tiberius**

9. Who was Romulus Augustulus? **the last Roman emperor in the West**
   - B1: Who was the philosopher emperor? **Marcus Aurelius**
   - B2: Which emperor fiddled while Rome burned? **Nero**

10. Which word, because of its meaning, does not belong with the others? *gerere, facere, discedere, agere* **discedere**
    - B1: Which word, because of its meaning, does not belong with the others? *mons, tumulus, agger, collis, mare* **mare**
    - B2: Which word, because of its meaning, does not belong with the others? *digitus, manus, domus, pes* **domus**

(cont.)

11. For the verb *do, dare* in the future perfect tense, active voice, indicative mood, give the third person plural. **dederint**
   - B1: Make *dederint* passive. **dati erunt OR datae erunt OR data erunt**
   - B2: Make *dederint* pluperfect. **dederant**

12. Complete this analogy: Epimetheus:Pandora:: ______:Aurora. **Tithonus**
   - B1: Tithonus:______::Arachne:spider. **grasshopper**
   - B2: Tithonus:grasshopper:Lycaon:______. **wolf**

13. In what year did the Romans defeat Pyrrhus, thereby becoming mistress of Italy? **275 B.C.**
   - B1: What are the dates of the First Punic War? **264–241 B.C.**
   - B2: By what year was Rome the mistress of the Mediterranean world? **133 B.C.**

14. Where was the Temple of Saturn located? **in the Forum**
   - B1: Where was the Pantheon located? **in the Campus Martius**
   - B2: Where was the *Aerarium* located? **in the Forum**

15. Which word does not have the same Latin root as the others? transfer, translate, latitude, confer **latitude**
   - B1: Which word does not have the same Latin root as the others? imply, comply, pliable, placate **placate**
   - B2: Which word does not have the same Latin root as the others? translucent, luxury, lucidity, luculent **luxury**

16. Make *mulier* accusative. **mulierem**
   - B1: Make *mulierem* plural. **mulieres**
   - B2: Make *mulieres* ablative. **mulieribus**

17. *Responde Latine in casu nominativo.* Where, very specifically, would a Roman have gone to hear a public speaker? **rostrum OR rostra**
   (Do not accept an answer beginning with "the.")
   - B1: *Responde Latine:* Where would a Roman have gone to see an athlete exercising? **Campus Marius OR ad Campum Martium**
   - B2: *Responde Latine:* Where would a Roman have gone, very specifically, to take a cold plunge? **frigidarium OR ad frigidarium OR in frigidarium**

18. Who does not belong in this group: Athena, Poseidon, Aphrodite, Hera? **Poseidon**
   - B1: Who does not belong in this group: Athena, Hestia, Artemis, Aphrodite? **Aphrodite**
   (She is not virginal.)
   - B2: Who does not belong in this group: Eros, Aphrodite, Ares, Iris? **Iris**
   (She is not one of the family.)

19. Complete this analogy: *toga candida*:a man running for office::*tunica recta*:______. **a bride**
   - B1: *tunica recta*:a bride::*toga picta*:______. **a victorious general**
   - B2: *toga picta*:a victorious general:______:a boy after his sixteenth birthday. **toga virilis**

20. What case follows the Latin adjective *gratus*? **dative**
   - B1: What case follows the Latin verb *credo*? **dative**
   - B2: What case follows the Latin verb *praesum*? **dative**

Novice Certamen
Round III

1. Complete the following analogy. *filia:filabus::matre:_______.* **matribus**
   - B1: *...rex:reges::senator:_______.* **senatores**
   - B2: *...diebus:die::solibus:_______.* **sole**

2. Give a synonum for *laetus.* **beatus, felix, fortunatus**
   - B1: Give an antonum for *laetus.* **miser, infelix**
   - B2: Give an antonym for *angustus.* **latus**

3. What case follows the preposition *prae*? **ablative**
   - B1: What case follows the preposition *in* when it means "into"? **accusative**
   - B2: What case dlows the preposition *intra*? **accusative**

4. What word does not belong in this group because of its meaning? *leo, tigris, elephantus, scutum* **scutum**
   - B1: *...vir, femina, virtus, puer* **virtus**
   - B2: *...caput, pes, bracchium, canis* **canis**

5. Give the third principal part of *pono.* **posui**
   - B1: ...of *maneo.* **mansi**
   - B2: ...of *iuvo.* **iuvi**

6. Give the Latin adjective and its meaning from which we derive *clarify.* **clarus (bright/clear)**
   - B1: Give the Latin noun and its meaning from which we derive *translucent.* **lux (light)**
   - B2: Give the Latin noun and its meaning from which we derive *gladiator.* **gladius (sword)**

7. Give the fourth principal part of *maneo.* **mansum/mansurum**
   - B1: ...of *sto.* **statum/staturum**
   - B2: ...of *habeo.* **habitum**

8. What derivative of *vir* means "manly"? **virile**
   - B1: ...of *lux* means "transparent"? **translucent**
   - B2: ...of *bos* means "like a cow"? **bovine**

9. What case follows the Latin adjective *carus*? **dative**
   - B1: *...gratus?* **dative**
   - B2: *...idoneus?* **dative**

10. Which man dear to Aurora turned into a grasshopper? **Tithonus**
    - B1: Which goddess caused Arachne's metamorphosis? **Athena/Minerva**
    - B2: What did Arachne turn into? **a spider**

11. Complete the following analogy. Aeneas:Creusa::Hector:_______. **Andromache**
    - B1: Aeneas:Anchises::Hector:_______. **Priam**
    - B2: Lavina:Aeneas::Andromache:_______. **Helenus**

(cont.)

12. What was the job of the *nomenclator*? **to call out names to his patron**
   - B1: ...of the *paedagogus*? **to lead the boy to school**
   - B2: ...of the *pistor*? **to bake**

13. What volcano destroyed Pompeii? **Vesuvius**
   - B1: Give the month, day, and year of the destructive eruption. **August 24, A.D. 79**
   - B2: What were the two other cities destroyed by the same eruption? **Herculaneum and Stabiae**

14. What salute, in Latin, did the gladiators give before beginning to fight? **Nos morituri te salutamus.**
   - B1: What formulaic speech did a bride make to her groom? **Ego tu Gaius, ego Gaia.**
   - B2: Who is reputed by Shakespeare to have said, "Et tu, Brute"? **Gaius Julius Caesar**

15. Give the month, day and year of the founding of Rome. **April 21, 753 B.C.**
   - B1: ...of the death of Julius Caesar. March 15, 44 B.C.
   - B2:. What was the name of that day in March, according to Romans' calendar? **the Ides**

16. What is the meaning for the abbreviation "N.B."? **nota bene (note well)**
   - B1: ...of "i.e."? **id est (that is)**
   - B2: ...of "e.g."? **exempli gratia (for example)**

17. What bridge did Horatio defend? **the pons Sublicius**
   - B1: Of what material was the *pons Sublicius* made? **wood**
   - B2.: What part of his body did Gaius Mucius lose? **his right hand**

18. What was the *culina* in a Roman home? **the kitchen**
   - B1: What was the *triclinium*? **the dining room**
   - B2: What was the *cubiculum*? **a bedroom**

19. In what year did Caesar cross the Rubicon? **49 B.C.**
   - B1: What city fell to the Turks in A.D. 1453? **Constantinople**
   - B2:. What city did the Romans capture in A.D. 70? **Jerusalem**

20. Differentiate in meaning between *via* and *villa*. **road/street; farmhouse**
   - B1: ...between *mox* and *nox*. **soon and night**
   - B2: ...between *mons* and *mens*. **mountain and mind**

Novice Certamen

Final Round

1. What Latin noun gives us *intramural*? **murus**
   - B1: What Latin noun gives us *pedestrian*? **pes**
   - B2: What Latin noun gives us *interstellar*? **stella**

2. In what year did Constantine defeat Maxentius? **A.D. 312**
   - B1: In what year was the Arch of Constantine erected in Rome? **A.D. 315**
   - B2: What city in what is today Turkey did Constantine establish? **Constantinople/Istanbul**

3. For the verb *habeo*, give the third principal part. **habui**
   - B1: Give the fourth principal part of *dico*. **dictus/a/um**
   - 8 B2: Give the fourth principl part of *tango*. **tactus/a/um**

4. Conjugate the verb *amo* in the present active. **amo, amas, amat, amamus, amatis, amant**
   - B1: Make *amat* passive. **amatur**
   - B2: Translate *amatur*. **he/she/it is loved**

5. Say in Latin, "We love Latin." **Latinam amamus.**
   - B1: What case is *Latinam*? **accusative**
   - B2: Make the sentence negative. **Latinam non amamus.**

6. What Latin word introduces a question expecting the answer of "no"? **num**
   - B1: What Latin word introduces a question expecting the answer of "yes"? **nonne**
   - B2: What does the enclitic *-que* mean? **and**

7. Which hero had to sow dragons' teeth in order to obtain a unique fleece? **Jason**
   - B1: Which woman helped Jason in his adventures? **Medea**
   - B2: What did Medea do in revenge to her children? **She killed them.**

8. What is the case of *puellarum*? **genitive**
   - B1: Make *puellarum* ablative. **puellis**
   - B2: Make *puellis* dative. **puellis**

9. Who was turned into a weeping stone? **Niobe**
   - B1: Why was she turned into a weeping stone? **because she made fun of Leto/Latona for having only two children**
   - B2: Who were the children of Leto/Latona? **Apollo and Artemis/Apollo and Diana**

10. How many emperors were there in A.D. 69? **four**
    - B1: Name one of these four emperors. **Nero, Galba, Otho, Vitellius**
    - B2: Name one more. **Nero, Galba, Otho, Vitellius**

11. Define *vigenti*. **twenty**
    - B1: *Quot sunt viginti minus duo?* **duodeviginti**
    - B2: *Quot sunt sex et septem?* **tredecim**

12. Which Greek hero had a problem with his heel? **Achilles**
    - B1: According to tradition, who killed Achilles in the Trojan War? **Paris**
    - B2: Who was the mother of Paris? **Hecuba**

(cont.)

13. Decline *ego*. **ego, mei, mihi, me, me**
- B1: Make *ego* plural. **nos**
- B2: Decline *tu*. **tu, tui, tibi, te, te**

14. Give an antonym for *malus*. **bonus**
- B1: Give an antonym for *miser*. **felix/fortunatus/beatus**
- B2: Give an antonym for *foedus*. **pulcher**

15. Who was the first husband of Ocatvian's sister Octavia Minor? **Marcellus**
- B1: Who was her second husband? **Marcus Antonius/Mark Antony**
- B2: What poet wrote in the *Aeneid* about Octavia Minor's late son? **Vergil**

16. For the verb *venio* give the first person singular, perfect tense, active voice. **veni**
- B1: Give the same form for *video*. **vidi**
- B2: Give the same form for *vinco*. **vici**

17. Define the derivative *hibernate*. **(to) sleep through the winter**
- B1: Define the derivative *estivate*. **(to) sleep through the summer**
- B2: Give the Latin for "to sleep." **dormire**

18. What Latin word, the name of a number, gives us the derivative *decimal*? **decem**
- B1: Make *decem* an ordinal number. **decimus/a/um**
- B2: What Latin number represents half of *decem*. **quinque**

19. Which of the following was not a Trojan: Priam, Cassandra, Odysseus, Aeneas? **Odysseus**
- B1: Which of the following was not a Greek: Paris, Agamemnon, Menelaus, Nestor? **Paris**
- B2: Which of the following was not a Roman: Casear, Scribonia, Cleopatra, Agrippina? **Cleopatra**

20. We have liked today's contests. How would you say contests in Latin for that sentence? **certamina**
- B1: We have played four rounds of *certamen*. How would you say "four" in Latin in that sentence? **quattuor**
- B2: This is the fourth *certamen*. How would you say in Latin "fourth" in that sentence? **quartum**

Intermediate Certamen

Round I

1. What river did Caesar cross in 49 B.C.? **the Rubicon**
   - B1: In what month of 49 B.C. did he cross the Rubicon? **January**
   - B2: In what month of 44 B.C. did Caesar die? **March**

2. Give the fourth principal part of *pario*. **partus/a/um**
   - B1: Give the fourth principal part of *spargo*. **sparsus/a/um**
   - B2: Give the fourth principal part of *aufero*. **ablatus/a/um**

3. Give the Latin noun and its meaning from which we derive *defenestration*. **fenestra (window)**
   - B1: The name of what English month is connected to a Latin noun meaning "door"? **January**
   - B2: What Latin noun naming a piece of furniture is also the name of an organization for geniuses? **mensa**

4. *Quis erat pater Creusae Paridisque?* **Priamus**
   - B1: *Quis erat Priami uxor, mater Creusae Paridisque?* **Hecuba**
   - B2: *Quis Creusam in matrimonium duxit?* **Aeneas**

5. What two uses of the dative comprise the double dative? **dative of reference AND dative of purpose**
   - B1: What type of dative is used with passive periphrastic? **dative of agent**
   - B2: Which of the following verbs is <u>not</u> followed by the dative case: *persuadeo, credo, tango,* or *pareo?* **tango**

6. What is the meaning of the Latin phrase *non compos mentis?* **not sound of mind/not of sound mind**
   - B1: What is the meaning of the legal term *et ux.?* **and wife**
   - B2: In what type of case would a judge release someone *ex vinculis matrimoni?* **a divorce case**

7. What term describes a verb that has or may have a direct object? **transitive**
   - B1: What term describes a verb that does not or may not have a direct object? **instransitive**
   - B2: What term describes a verb that is passive in form but active in meaning? **deponent**

8. Define *sterno*. **smoothe, pave, lay low**
   - B1: Define *aster*. **star**
   - B2: Define *ter*. **three times**

9. In the conflict with the canton of the Tigurini, whose death did Caesar feel he was avenging? **that of his father-in-law's grandfather/ that of Lucius Calpurnius Piso**
   - B1 To what larger group did the Tigurini belong? **the Helvetii/Helvetians**
   - B2: Into how many cantons was the Helvetian state divided? **four**

10. The Carthaginians originally came to Africa from Phoenicia. What do we call the area of ancient Phoenicia today? **Lebanon**
    - B1: Dido was told she could have all the land she could cover with what? **a bull's hide**
    - B2: What does *Carthago* mean? **New Town**

(cont.)

11. Which word does not belong with the others because of its meaning: *gladius, ensis, pilum,* or *castra?* **castra**
- B1: Which word does not belong with the others because of its meaning: *ebur, ferrum, oppidum,* or *gladius?* **oppidum**
- B2: Which word does not belong with the others because of its meaning: *civis, civitas, gens,* or *urbs?* **civis**

12. For the verb *moneo* give the third person plural, imperfect tense, passive voice, subjunctive mood. **monerentur**
- B1: Make *monerentur* pluperfect. **moniti essent**
- B2: Make *moniti essent* present. **moneantur**

13. Make *celer* an adverb. **celeriter**
- B1: Make *potens* an adverb. **potenter**
- B2: Make *audax* an adverb. **audacter**

14. Give the Latin noun and its meaning from which we derive *celerity.* **celeritas (speed)**
- B1: Give the Latin adjective and its meaning from which we derive *clarity.* **clarus (clear, bright, famous)**
- B2: Give the Latin verb and its meaning from which we derive *lacrimose.* **lacrima (tear)**

15. Which word does not belong with the others because of tense: *eram, amabas, fueram, amaretur,* or *ferebam?* **fueram**
- B1: Which word does not belong with the others because of its gender: *ferrum, corpus, mare,* or *equus.* **equus**
- B2: Which word does not belong with the others because of its case: *puellam, templum, corporum,* or *montem?* **corporum**

16. For the noun *lux,* give the genitive plural. **lucum**
- B1: For the noun *mons* give the genitive plural. **montium**
- B2: For the noun *manus* give the genitive plural. **manuum**

17. If a Roman boy said to you, *"Esurio,"* what would you give him? **food**
- B1: If a Roman boy said to you, *"Sitio,"* what would you give him? **something to drink**
- B2: If a Roman boy said to you, *"Fessum sum,"* what would you suggest he do? **go to sleep/get some rest**

18. Which Greek god led the souls of the dead to the underworld? **Hermes**
- B1: Which Greek goddess is known as the Hera of the underworld? **Persephone**
- B2: Which Greek goddess is the goddess of crafts, warfare, and wisdom? **Athena/ Pallas Athene**

19. What case follows the Latin verb *parco*? **dative**
- B1: What case follows the Latin verb *noceo*? **dative**
- B2: What case follows the Latin verb *fruor*? **ablative**

20. Differentiate in meaning between *nomen* and *numen.* **name and spirit/godhead/divinity**
- B1: Differentiate in meaninq between *fero* and *gero.* **bring/bear/carry and wear/wage/carry**
- B2: Differentiate in meaning between *mox* and *nox.* **soon and night**

Intermediate Certmen

Round II

1. After what campaign did Caesar receive the title *imperator?* **the Helvetian campaign**
   - B1: By what title was a general styled before he won his first major campaign? **dux**
   - B2: What Helvetian leader married his daughter to Dumnorix? **Orgetorix**

2. Give the first principal part of *sparsum.* **spargo**
   - B1: Give the first principal part of *sublatum.* **tollo**
   - B2: Give the first principal part of *partum.* **pario**

3. Give the Latin verb and its meaning from which we derive *concurrent.* **curro (run)**
   - B1: What Latin preposition combines with *curro* to form *concurrent?* **cum**
   - B2: What is the meaning of *cum* when it followed by a noun or pronoun in the ablative? **with**

4. *Quis erat mater Romuli Remique?* **Rhea Silvia**
   - B1: *Quis erat Romuli Remique pater?* **Mars**
   - B2: *Quod animal Romulum Remumque aluit?* **lupa**

5. What case in Latin shows means? **ablative**
   - B1: What case in Latin shows accompaniment? **ablative**
   - B2: What case in Latin shows manner? **ablative**

6. What is the meaning of the Latin phrase *mens sana in corpore sano?* **a sound mind in a sound body**
   - B1: What is the meaning of the Latin phrase *ex libris?* **from the books (of)**
   - B2: Say in Latin, "out of many, one." **e pluribus unum/us/a**

7. What case in Latin is used to show price? **ablative**
   - B1: What case in Latin is used to show definite value? **genitive**
   - B2: What case in Latin is used to show duration of time? **accusative**

8. Define *campus.* **plain/field**
   - B1: Define *castra.* **camp**
   - B2: Define *casa.* **house/cottage/hut**

9. What Roman leader and dictator was born in 102 or 100 B.C. in the month which now bears his name? **(Gaius Julius) Caesar**
   - B1: What Roman dictator left his plow to assume that post? **Cinncinatus**
   - B2: What Latin verb gives us the word *dictator?* **dico**

10. What was the market place of Athens? **the Agora**
    - B1: What was the market place of Rome? **the Forum**
    - B2: What was the name given to the speaker's platform in the Roman Forum? **the rostra**

11. Which word does not belong with the others because of a point of grammar: *sum, eram, amor,* or *monetur?* **monetur**
    - B1: Which word does not belong with the others because of a point of grammar: *amor, proficiscor, polliceor, or loquor?* **amor**
    - B2: Which word does not belong with the others because of a point of grammar: *rex, mons, pax, or civis?* **pax**

(cont.)

12. Give the third person singular, passive voice, indicative mood of *do*. **datur**
- B1: Make *datur* subjunctive. **detur**
- B2: Make *detur* active. **det**

13. Give the genitive of *maria*. **marium**
- B1: Give the genitive of *lux*. **lucis**
- B2: Give the genitive of *cornu*. **cornus**

14. Give the Latin nouns and their meanings from which we derive *cornucopiae*. **cornu (horn) and copia (supply/plenty)**
- B1: What is the meaning of *copia* in the plural? **troops**
- B2: What is the meaning of *castra* in the singular? **fort**

15. Make *fuisti* pluperfect. **fueras**
- B1: Make *fueras* future perfect. **fueris**
- B2: Make *fueris* present. **es**

16. Define *lux*. **light**
- B1: Define *lugeo*. **mourn**
- B2: Define *nux*. **nut**

17. What would you do if your teacher said, "*Surge!*"? **rise**
- B1: What would you do if your teacher said, "*Lege Latine*"? **read in Latin**
- B2: What would you do if your teacher said, "*Ambula ad fenestram*"? **walk to the window**

18. *Quis erat mater Propserpinae?* **Ceres**
- B1: *Quis Proserpinam abduxit?* **Pluto**
- B2: *Quod regnum regnabatur a Plutone?* **Tartarus**

19. What color was the bride's veil? **yellow/saffron/red/flame colored**
- B1: Into how many locks was a bride's hair parted? **six**
- B2: What was used to part her hair? **a spear**

20. Where in Rome would you have heard "*Nos morituri te salutamus*"? **in the arena**
- B1: Where in Rome would you have heard Cicero deliver an oration to the people? **in the Forum/ at the Rostrum**
- B2: At what event in Rome would you have heard a young woman say, "*Ubi tu Gaius, ego Gaia*"? **at a wedding**

Intermediate Certamen
Round III

1. *Quot labores perfecti sunt ab Hercule?* **duodecim**
   - B1: *Quot capita Cerbero erant?* **trina/tria**
   - B2: *Quot Musae erant?* **novem**

2. For the verb *proficiscor* give the present infinitive. **proficisci**
   - B1: For the verb *conor* give the present imperative singular. **conare**
   - B2: Make *conare* plural. **conamini**

3. What two cases may follow the Latin verb *potior*? **genitive and ablative**
   - B1: What case follows the Latin verb *credo* when the object is a person? **dative**
   - B2: What case follows the Latin verb *credo* when the object is what is believed? **accusative**

4. What did Atalanta and Hippomenes become after their metamorphoses? **lions**
   - B1: What did Baucis and Philemon become? **trees**
   - B2: What did Arachne become? **a spider**

5. Which of the following is not a part of a Roman *domus*: *triclinium, alae, cornua, culina*? **cornua**
   - B1: What room of a *domus* was the master's study? **the tablinum**
   - B2: What room of a *domus* takes its name from a Latin adjective meaning "black." **the atrium**

6. What is the gender of *pax*? **feminine**
   - B1: What is the gender of *lux*? **feminine**
   - B2: What is the gender of *mons*? **masculine**

7. Interpret the idiom *castra ponere.* **to pitch camp**
   - B1: Interpret the idiom *multa nocte.* **late at night**
   - B2: Interpret the idiom *magnum iter.* **a forced march**

8. Upon what object might one fine the word *pinxit.* **a painting**
   - B1: Upon what object might one find the word *obiit*? **a tombstone**
   - B2: What might you have in your wallet having the the Latin sentence "Annuit coeptis"? **a dollar bill**

9. We all know that Gaul was divided into three parts. Name the people who inhabited each part. **the Belgae/Belgians, the Galli/Gauls/Celts, the Aquitani/Aquitanians**
   - B1: Of which of the peoples was Vercingetorix a king? **the Gauls**
   - B2: Where did Vercingetorix die? **in Rome**

10. Differentiate in meaning among *nos, vos,* and *nox.* **we/us, you, and night**
    - B1: Differentiate in meaning among *pro, per,* and *post.* **for/on behalf of; through; and after/behind**
    - B2: Differentiate in meaning among *casa, causa,* and *casus.* **hut/cottage/house; reason/cause; and chance/misfortune/fall**

(cont.)

11. Which of the following would have a verb in the subjunctive: a *cum* concessive clause, an indirect statement, a passive periphrastic? **a cum concessive clause**
- B1: In a *cum* concessive, how does a reader interpret *cum*? **although**
- B2: Name another type of *cum* clause with a subjunctive verb. **causal/temporal**

12. Give the second person plural, present tense, active voice subjunctive mood of *dono.* **donetis**
- B1: Make *donetis* passive **donemini**
- B2: Make *donemini* pluperfect. **donati/ae/a essetis**

13. Interpret the idiom *prima luce.* **at dawn**
- B1: Interpret the idiom *iter facere.* **to travel/march**
- B2: Interpret the idiom *castra movere.* **to break camp**

14. What part of his body did Gaius Mucius lose? **his right hand**
- B1: How did he lose it? **by burning**
- B2: What king had he gone to kill when he lost his hand? **Lars Porsenna**

15. What modern Italian city's name means "new city"? **Naples**
- B1: What modern Italian city acquires its name from the Latin word for "flower"? **Florence**
- B2: Which of those two cities is nearer to Pompeii? **Naples**

16. Give the Latin noun which originally meant ivory but later named a mammal. **elephantus**
- B1: What mammal would a Roman have called balaena? **a whale**
- B2: What mammal would a Roman have called cameleopardis? **a giraffe**

17. Which of the following does not belong with the others because of its meaning: *quercus, ficus, morus,* or *mus*? **mus**
- B1: Define *mus.* **mouse**
- B2: What do the other words have in common? **They name trees./ They are second declension feminine.**

18. What declension of nouns has a sub-class called i-stem? **third**
- B1: What conjugation of verbs has a sub-class called io-verbs? **third**
- B2: To what declension do comparative adjectives belong? **third**

19. Compare *bonum.* **bonum, melius, optimum**
- B1: Compare *mala.* **mala, peior, pessima**
- B2: Make *peior* an adverb. **peius**

20. Who abducted Persephone? **Hades**
- B1: Who abducted Helen? **Paris**
- B2: Who abducted Europa? **Zeus/Jupiter**

Intermediate Certamen

Final Round

1. Who was the mother of Minos? **Europa**
   - B1: What was Minos' island kingdom? **Crete**
   - B2: What city was the capital of his kingdom? **Knossos**

2. *Quod flumen fluit per Romam?* **Tiber**
   - B1: *Quot insulae sunt in flumine quod fluit per Romam?* **una**
   - B2: *Qui deus habebat templum in insula in hoc flumine?* **Asclepias**

3. According to its Latin roots, what does *vinegar* literally mean? **sharp/sour wine**
   - B1: According to its Latin roots, what does *perfect* literally mean: **do completely/finish, done completely/finished**
   - B2: According to its Latin roots, what does *translated* literally mean? **brought/carried across**

4. I am going to read a Latin sentence to you twice and then ask you a question about it in Latin to which you must respond correctly in Latin.
   "Caesar flumen transire constituit." Quis flumen transibit? **Caesar**
   - B1: *Quam rem Caesar transibit?* **flumen**
   - B2: *Quid faciet Caesar?* **flumen transibit**

5. Besides on a bovine quadruped or in a battle formation, where might a Roman have seen *cornua*? **on a scroll**
   - B1: Besides on a nautical vessel, where might a Roman have seen *rostra*? **in the Forum/ at the speakers' platform**
   - B2: Besides on an elephant, where might Aeneas or Pyramus have seen *ebur*? **on his scabbard**

6. What did Jason have to sow and then conquer the products thereof? **dragon's teeth**
   - B1: What was the name of Jason's ship? **the Argo**
   - B2: What relative of hers did Medea sacrifice in order help Jason? **her brother**

7. *Qui rex Thebae patrem suum necavit et matrem suam in matrimonium duxit?* **Oedipus**
   - B1: *Quot liberi erant huic regi Thebae?* **quattuor**
   - B2: *Qui vates hunc regem monebat?* **Tiresias**

8. For the verb *maneo* give the first person plural, imperfect tense, active voice, subjunctive mood. **maneremus**
   - B1: Make *maneremus* present. **maneamus**
   - B2: Make *maneamus* perfect. **manserimus**

9. In indirect statement, what tense of the infinitive is used if the time of the indirect statement is the same time as the "verb of the head." **present**
   - B1: What tense is used if the time of the indirect statement has been before the time of the "verb of the head"? **perfect**
   - B2: What case is used for the subject of an indirect statement? **accusative**

10. Besides the genitive, what case may be used to show possession? **dative**
    - B1: What is the only one of the five major cases in Latin that is never an object of some kind? **nominative**
    - B2: What case follows the preposition *sine*? **ablative**

(cont.)

11. Who am I? I was nursed by the goat Amalthea and hung in a tree so that my father couldn't find me. Later I overthrew my father. The Romans called me Jupiter? **Zeus**
- B1: Who am I? I had a twin brother whose name means the opposite of mine. For a so-called crime I committed I was chained to a rock. **Prometheus**
- B2: Who am I? My mother was seduced by Zeus. Hera sent snakes to strangle my brother while we were in the cradle. My twin later performed twelve labors. **Iphicles**

12. Define *iustitia*. **justice**
- B1: Define *ius*. **law/soup/gravy**
- B2: Define *iuro*. **swear**

13. Give the genitive and gender of *lex*. **legis, feminine**
- B1: Give the genitive and gender of *lux*. **lucis, feminine**
- B2: Give the genitive and gender of *flumen*. **fluminis, neuter**

14. How many laws were contained on the tables? **twelve**
- B1: In what year were these laws formulated? **451 B.C.**
- B2: How many men worked to formulate them? **ten**

15. What maiden, threatened by a sea-monster, was saved by Perseus? **Andromeda**
- B1: Who was Andromeda's mother? **Cassiopia**
- B2: Who had sent the sea-monster? **Poseidon**

16. How many praetors were elected annually? **eight**
- B1: How many quaestors were elected annually? **twelve**
- B2: How many consuls were elected annually? **two**

17. Which Roman consul refused a bribe made by Pyrrhus? **Fabricius**
- B1: Which Roman jumped into an abyss in order to save Rome? **Mettius/Mettius Curtius**
- B2: Which Roman consul killed his sons when they wanted the Tarquins returned to Rome? **Brutus**

18. What is a *modus vivendi*? **a way of living**
- B1: What is a *modus operandi*? **a way of operating**
- B2: What is a *sine qua non*? **something one cannot do without/something indispensable**

19. Complete the following analogy: *dico* is to *narro* as *accedo* is to ________. **appropinquo/adeo**
- B1: Complete the following analogy: *navis* is to in *mari* as *currus* is to ________. **in via/in circo**
- B2: Complete the following analogy: *dux* is to *exercitum* as *gubernator* is to ________. **navem**

20. Whom did Caesar defeat at the Battle of Zela in 47 B.C.? **Pharnaces**
- B1: The remains of whose forces did Caesar defeat at the Battle of Thapsus in 46 B.C.? **Pompey's**
- B2: At what battle in 45 B.C. did Caesar wipe out the army led by Pompey's sons? **the Battle of Munda**

Advanced Certamen
Round I

1. What is the third principal part of *parco*? **peperci**
   - B1: What is the third principal part of *tollo*? **sustuli**
   - B2: What is the third principal part of *sterno*? **stratus/a/um**

2. What is the Latin noun and its meaning from which we derive *legislature*? **lex (law)**
   - B1: What is the Latin noun with its meaning from which we derive *remuneration*? **munus (gift, duty, show)**
   - B2: What is the Latin noun with its meaning from which we derive *commensurate*? **mensa (table)**

3. Who wanted to make a favorite race horse consul? **Nero**
   - B1: What was the name of the horse? **Incitatus**
   - B2: Did Nero persecute Christians in the Colosseum? **No**

4. Who was Hera's messenger, the goddess of the rainbow? **Iris**
   - B1: What god was the messenger of Zeus? **Hermes**
   - B2: What was his Latin name? **Mercurius**

5. What was a slaves's *pelicula*? **his savings AND/OR personal property**
   - B1: What was the job of the *nomenclator*? **to tell his master people's names**
   - B2: What was the job of a *coqua*? **to cook**

6. What consul delivered four orations in 63 B.C. against Lucius Sergius Catilina? **Cicero**
   - B1: What name is given to the orations Cicero delivered against Mark Antony? **the *Philippics***
   - B2: What Latin preposition is used in the title of an oration against someone? **in**

7. Define *coram*. **in front of/before the face of/in public**
   - B1: Define *instar*. **in the likeness of**
   - B2: Define *infra*. **below**

8. What adverb formed from *parvus* means "too little"? **parum**
   - B1: What is the comparative of *magnopere*? **magis**
   - B2: What is the comparative of *alte*? **altius**

9. Give the Latin noun and its English meaning from which we derive *pioneer*. **pes (foot)**
   - B1: The name of what chess piece is also derived from *pes*? **pawn**

   8 B2: What derivative of *pes* names one who sells things door-to-door? **peddler**

10. Which emperor conducted a building program in Athens and built a wall in Britain? **Hadrian**
    - B1: Who was Hadrian's immediate predecessor? **Trajan**
    - B2: Did Hadrian lessen or expand the boundaries of the Empire as they had been under Trajan? **lessened them**

11. Translate into Latin the phrase for "good sailors" in the sentence "We gave the money to the good sailors." **nautis bonis**
    - B1: Make *nautis bonis* singular. **nautae bono**
    - B2: Make *nautae bono* accusative. **nautam bonum**

(cont.)

12. Which preposition does <u>not</u> belong with the others because it is followed by a different case: *coram, per, infra,* or *ad*? **coram**
   - B1: What case patterns with *prae*? **ablative**
   - B2: What case patterns with *sub* when there is motion implied? **accusative**

13. Using the verb *fruor* say in Latin, "I enjoy books." **Fruor libris.**
   - B1: Using the verb *credo* say in Latin, "I believe you." **Credo tibi.**
   - B2: Using the verb *persuadeo* say in Latin, "He had persuaded me." **Mihi persuaserat.**

14. Who penned the line *"Exegi monumentum aere perennius."* **Horace**
   - B1: What did Horace mean as the *monumentum* in that line? **his poetry**
   - B2: What Muse did Horace mention in that poem? **Melpomene**

15. What are the two possible tenses of *dederint*? **future perfect and perfect**
   - B1: What tense is *poterat*? **imperfect**
   - B2: What tense if *praefuerat*? **pluperfect**

16. What son of Jupiter Hammon appears in Book IV of the *Aeneid*? **Iarbas**
   - B1: Who is Barce, who also appears in this book. **the nurse of Sychaeus/ of Dido's first husband**
   - B2: Who sends Iris to cut a lock of Dido's hair? **Juno**

17. What service did Ganymede perform for the deities? **He was the cupbearer.**
   - B1: Whom had Ganymede replaced as cupbearer? **Hebe**
   - B2: Who was Hebe's mother? **Juno**

18. What was the fictional name of Catullus' mistress about whom he wrote poems? **Lesbia**
   - B1: What was probably her real name? **Clodia/Claudia**
   - B2: What Greek poetess had written poems which Catullus later imitated? **Sappho**

19. Which king of Rome established the Roman religion? **Numa Pompilius**
   - B1: Which dictator of Rome revised the calendar? **Caesar**
   - B2: Which dictator of Rome returned to his plow when the crisis ended? **Cincinnatus**

20. I am going to read to you a Latin sentence twice and then ask you a question about it to which you must respond correctly in Latin. *"Hodie Romam ibo ut Ciceronem audiam." Quo ibo hodie?* **Romam**
   - B1: *Cur Romam ibo?* **ut Ciceronem audiam**
   - B2: Which of the following is another way to state *ut Ciceronem audiam*: *Ciceronis audiendi gratia, audire Ciceronem, ut Ciceronem audivisset?* **Ciceronis audiendi gratia**

Advanced Certamen
Round II

1. Give the fourth principal part of *aufero*. **ablatus/a/us**
   - B1: Give the fourth principal part of *admoneo*. **admonitus/a/um**
   - B2: Give the fourth principal part of *fallo*. **falsus/a/um**

2. Give the Latin verb and its meaning from which we derive *obnoxious*. **noceo (harm)**
   - B1: Give the Latin verb and its meaning from which we derive *illegible*. **lego (read)**
   - B2: Give the Latin verb and its meaning from which we derive *occurrence*. **curro (run)**

3. What poisoned Claudius? **mushrooms**
   - B1: What does the name *Claudius* mean? **lame/crippled**
   - B2: What would all daughters of a man with the *nomen* of Claudius be named? **Claudia**

4. *Quis Medusam necavit?* **Perseus**
   - B1: *Quis Minotaurum necavit?* **Theseus**
   - B2: *Quis Pegasum peperit?* **Medusa**

5. What was a *strigil* used for? **for scraping oil off the body (in the baths)**
   - B1: What was the *frigidarium* in the baths? **the cold room**
   - B2: The Roman baths were much like which of the following modern institutions: a country club, a shoppinq mall, or a sports arena? **a country club**

6. Who were the first consuls at Rome? **Brutus and Collatinus**
   - B1: Whose death led to the expulsion of the kings and the creation of the consulate? **Lucretia's**
   - B2: The relative of what king of Rome caused Lucretia to commit suicide? **Lucius Tarquinius Superbus**

7. Define *pareo*. **obey**
   - B1: Define *par*. **equal**
   - B2: Define *pars*. **part/share/role**

8. What is the comparative of *idoneus?* **magis idoneus**
   - B1: What is the comparative of *bonum?* **melius**
   - B2: What is the superlative of *male?* **pessime**

9. Give the Latin noun and its meaning from which we derive *corpulent*. **corpus (body)**
   - B1: What is the meaning of *corpulent?* **fat**
   - B2: What is the meaning of the derivative *incorporeal*. **bodiless/without a body**

10. In what year was Jerusalem conquered and destroyed? **A.D. 70**
    - B1: Who was emperor in that year? **Titus**
    - B2: Who was emperor when the Colosseum was begun? **Vespasian**

11. Define the idiom *consilium capere*. **to form a plan/to adopt a plan**
    - B1: Define the idiom *vitam agere*. **to live**
    - B2: Define the idiom *in matronium ducere*. **to marry**

(cont.)

12. Which of the following verbs does not belong with the others: *fungor, vescor, polliceor, utor?* **polliceor**
   - B1: What is the meaning of *fungor?* **perform**
   - B2: What two cases can *potior* govern? **ablative and genitive**

13. What events were held in the Circus Maximus? **chariot races**
   - •8 B1: What did the Romans call the Colosseum? **the Flavian Amphitheater**
   - B2: In what year was the Flavian Amphitheater completed? **A.D. 80**

14. Differentiate in meaning between *pareo* and *pario.* **obey and give birth to**
   - B1: What case patterns with *pareo?* **dative**
   - B2: What is the fourth principal part of *pario?* **partus/a/um**

15. Give the Latin verb and its meaning from which we derive *desperate?* **spero (hope)**
   - B1: Give the Latin verb and its meaning from which we derive *transpose?* **pono (place/put)**
   - B2: Give the Latin verb and its meaning from which we derive *ablative?* **fero (bring/carry)**

16. What Latin word, which is spelled like the name in English for a female or mother horse, means "sea"? **mare**
   - B1: What Latin verb form sounds like the name in English for a young or small equine quadruped? **poni**
   - B2: What Latin word is spelled like the name of a rental car company in English? **avis**

17. What Roman died a few days into his seventh consulate? **Marius**
   - B1: What Roman dictator was described as having a complexion like mulberries sprinkled with meal? **Sulla**
   - B2: Who was the son-in-law and best friend of Augustus, the man he desired to succeed him? **Agrippa**

18. In which book of the *Aeneid* does Aeneas find the golden bough? **the sixth**
   - B1: In which book of the *Aeneid* does Turnus die? **the twelfth**
   - B2: In which book of the *Aeneid* does Aeneas' last encounter with Dido occur? **the sixth**

19. Which word does not pattern with the same case as the others: *credo, persuado, oblisviscor, gratus?* **obliviscor**
   - B1: What case patterns with *oblisviscor*? **genitive**
   - B2: What case patterns with the other words? **dative**

20. What two Roman emperors abdicated in 305? **Diocletian and Maximian**
   - B1: In what year did Maximian die? **310**
   - B2: Who was the husband of Maximian's daughter, Fausta? **Constantine**

Advanced Certamen

Round III

1. What is the fourth principal part of *tollo*? **sublatus/a/um**
   - B1: What is the fourth principal part of *scribo*? **scriptus/a/um**
   - B2: What is the fourth principal part of *parco*? **parsus/a/um**

2. Define *obliviscor*. **forget**
   - B1: Define *odium*. **hatred**
   - B2: Define *osculum*. **kiss**

3. At what battle did Constantine defeat Maxentius? **the battle at the Milvian Bridge**
   - B1: In what year did this battle occur? **312**
   - B2: Where did Constantine and Licinius meet to partition the Roman world? **Milan**

4. In the *Aeneid* there are several icons, works of art described in a work of art. Identify one of these icons. **the temple murals at Carthage, the doors of Apollo's temple at Cumae, Aeneas' shield, or Pallas' belt**
   - B1: What is the term for a poet's stopping the action of the plot to describe a place. This description often begins with "*Est locus.*" **ekphrasis**
   - B2: What figure of speech occurs when the two parts of a compound word are split by another word or other words? **tmesis**

5. "A Funny Thing Happened on the Way to the Forum" is based on two plays by what Roman? **Plautus**
   - B1: Plautus wrote great comedy, but what type of plays did Seneca write? **tragedies**
   - B2: Seneca was the tutor of what Roman emperor? **Nero**

6. The *novi poetae* modeled their style after the poets of what city? **Alexandria**
   - B1: Which of these was a *novus poeta:* Catullus, Vergil, or Ovid. **Catullus**
   - B2: What poet wrote a poem in which Chloe avoids the speaker like a fawn? **Horace**

7. What is the meaning of the phrase "*infra dig*"? **beneath one's dignity**
   - B1: What is the meaning of the phrase "*inter nos*"? **between/among us**
   - B2: What is the meaning of the phrase "*primus inter pares*"? **first among equals**

8. According to Caesar, who were the bravest of the Gauls? **the Belgians**
   - B1: According to Caesar, who surpassed the rest of the Gauls in courage? **the Helvetians**
   - B2: According to Caesar, what Helvetian was the noblest and richest? **Orgetorix**

9. Give the Latin origin of *volatile*. **volo/volare**
   - B1: Give the Latin origin of *fugitive*. **fugio/fugere**
   - B2: Give the Latin origin of *tenacious*. **teneo/tenere**

10. What are the three orders of Greek architecture? **Doric, Ionic, and Corinthian**
    - B1: Which of the three orders is characterized by a scroll? **the Ionic**
    - B2: The columns of how many of these three orders adorn the Colosseum? **(all) three**

11. Translate into Latin, "Caesar used to spare his enemies." **Caesar inimicis suis parcebat.**
    - B1: Using a deponent verb, translate into Latin "Caesar was speaking." **Caesar loquebatur.**
    - B2: Make *loquebatur* pluperfect. **locutus erat**

(cont.)

12. What case follows the Latin adjective *memor*? **genitive**
• B1: What case follows the Latin participle *oblitus*? **genitive**
• B2: What case follows the Latin verb *servio*? **dative**

13. In Cicero's words "*Quo usque tandem abutere ... patientia nostra*," what is the case of *patientia*? **ablative**
• B1: What is the tense of *abutere*? **future**
• B2: What are the person and number of *abutere* and what would be its more commonly used form? **second singular; *abuteris***

14. Which of the following was not a lyric poet: Propertius, Catullus, Terence, or Horace? **Terence**
• B1: What genre did Terence write? **tragedy**
• B2: What is the genre of Vergil's *Bucolics*? **pastoral poetry**

15. Make *amabatur* subjunctive. **amaretur**
• B1: Make *amaretur* pluperfect. **amatus esset**
• B2: Make *amatus esset* indicative. **amatus erat**

16. Which god appears in Book IV of the *Aeneid* to warn Aeneas? **Mercury**
• B1: Which goddesses in Book IV plot the marriage of Dido and Aeneas? **Juno and Venus**
• B2: Which goddess is reassured by Jupiter about the Trojans' future in Book I? **Venus**

17. On what island was the Minoan civilization? **Crete**
• B1: What island was Rome's first province? **Sicily**
• B2: What island did Claudius invade in A.D. 43? **Britain**

18. What animal is sacrificed to the spring of Bandusia? **a kid**
• B1: What insects played a large part in the *Georgics*? **bees**
• B2: What animal avoids Horace in his poem about the man who leads a pure life? **a wolf**

19. Which emperor renewed the persecution of Christians in 257? **Valerian**
• B1: Who ended the persecution of Christians in 260? **Gallienus**
• B2: Who became emperor in 268? **Claudius**

20. I am going to read to you a Latin sentence twice and then ask you a question about it to which you must respond correctly in Latin.
"Ego et frater meus eramus in nave ubi tempestas orta est."
Quis erat mecum ubi tempestas orta est? **frater (meus)**
• B1: *Quae res orta est?* **tempestas**
• B2: *Ubi eram ubi erat tempestas?* **in nave**

Advanced Certamen

Final Round

1. Make *magna* superlative. **maxima**
   - B1: Make *magnopere* superlative. **maxime**
   - B2: Make *idoneus* superlative. **maxime idoneus**

2. What is the Latin noun with its meaning from which we derive *eliminate?* **limen (threshold)**
   - B2: What is the Latin noun with its meaning from which we derive *voluptuary?* **voluptas (pleasure)**
   - B2: What is the Latin noun with its meaning from which we derive *salacious?* **sal (salt)**

3. *Quis imperator factus est post bellum cum Helvetiis?* **(Gaius Julius) Caesar**
   - B1: *Quis erat primus imperator Imperi Romani?* **Augustus**
   - B2: *Quis ultimus rex Romae fuit?* **Lucius Tarquinius Superbus**

4. What did the ceremony of manumission accomplish. **It freed a slave.**
   - B1: What type of ceremony was the *confarreatio?* **marriage**
   - B2: At what type of ceremony were *imagines* carried in a procession? **a funeral**

5. What is the meaning of the phrase *post mortem?* **after death**
   - B1: What is the meaning of the phrase *rigor mortis?* **the stiffness of death**
   - B2: What is the meaning of the word *excelsior?* **higher**

6. What is a *sine quo non*? something essential
   - B1: Wht part of speech is *sine*? preposition
   - B2: What part of speech is *non*? adverb

7. Define *instar.* **in the likeness/like**
   - B1: What case is used with *instar?* **genitive**
   - B2: What figure of speech does *instar* introduce? **simile**

8. What is the comparative of the adverb *late?* **latius**
   - B1: Make the adjective *utilis* superlative. **utillimus**
   - B2: Make the adjective *nobilis* superlative. **nobilissimus/a**

9. Give the month, day and year of the eruption of Mt. Vesuvius which destroyed Pompeii. **August 24, A.D. 79**
   - B1: Give the month, day and year of the founding of Rome. **April 21, 753 B.C.**
   - B2: Give the month, day and year of the death of Gaius Julius Caesar. **March 15, 44 B.C.**

10. Which of the following was never an emperor of Rome: Gaius Julius Caesar Augustus, Valerian, Gaius Julius Caesar? **Gaius Julius Caesar**
    - B1: Who of the following did not dedicate the *spolia opima:* Romulus, Marcellus, Gaius Julius Caesar? **Gaius Julius Caesar**
    - B2: Who of the following had four wives: Gaius Julius Caesar, Vergil, Tiberius? **Gaius Julius Caesar**

(cont.)

11. I am going to read a Latin sentence to you twice and then ask you a question about it to which you must respond correctly in Latin.
Cicero multas orationes habuit in Senatu et ad populum. Quibus rebus Cicero functus est? **orationibus**
- B1: *Ad quem orator locutus est?* **ad populum**
- B2: *Qua in re orator dicebat?* **in senatu**

12. Who of the following did not write satires: Juvenal, Horace or Livy? **Livy**
- B1: What genre did Livy write? **history**
- B2: What genre did Horace not write, odes or epics? **epics**

13. What do the verbs *utor* and *fungor* have in common, besides being deponent? **They govern the ablative.**
- B1: Name another verb which governs the ablative. **potior, fruor, vescor (or their compound)**
- B2: Name another. **potior, fruor, vescor (or their compound)**

14. Who is the reputed author of a poem about a mosquito? **Vergil**
- B1: What Roman satirist wrote about a city mouse and a country mouse? **Horace**
- B2: What Roman epic poet wrote about a goose who was rather like a watchdog? **Ovid**

15. What is the Latin grammatical exercise which requires one to list a verb in all its tenses in a certain person, number, voice and mood? **synopsis**
- B1: What is the term for the listing of a noun in all of its cases and numbers? **declension**
- B2: What is the term for the listing of a verb in a given tense, voice and mood with all its persons and numbers? **conjugation**

16. What is unique about the words *duo* and *ambo*? **They are dual in number.**
- B1: What two Latin nouns end in *-ul*? **consul and exsul**
- B2: What adverb meaning "from afar" ends in *-ul*? **procul**

17. Which of the following was not a son of Zeus: Perseus, Heracles or Romulus? **Romulus**
- B1: Who was the father of Cupid? **Mars**
- B2: Who was the sister of Cadmus whom Zeus seduced in the form of a bull? **Europa**

18. Which wind was Zephyrus? **the west wind**
- B1: Which wind was Notus? **the south wind**
- B2: Which wind was Africus? **the southwest wind**

19. Which of the following does not belong with the others because of its meaning: *tempestas, procellus, porcellus,* or *ventus?* **porcellus**
- B1: What is the name given to words like *porcellus, fraterculus* and *ocelli?* **diminutive(s)**
- B2: What is the meaning of *procellus?* **gust**

20. If a noun ends in the suffix *-men,* what are the last five letters in its genitive singular? **m i n i s**
- B1: What is the gender of all such nouns? **neuter**
- B2: What is the meaning of the suffix *-men?* **thing**

Chapter Nine

Endings

This chapter had its inception when my students and I one day tried to name all the possible "endings"—really final letters, I suppose, for third declension nouns. Amazingly, the students were able to come up with most of them by literally going through the alphabet and thinking of third declension nouns that ended with that letter. They then tried to think of other words with the same final letter and thus they reviewed vocabulary. I then added words they hadn't thought of.

Later, we tried to determine what the endings could tell us; for example, we deduced that all nouns ending in *-men* are third declension, neuter and have *-minis* for the genitive singular. Students also learned that most abstract nouns in this declension end in *-tas* or *-tudo* and are feminine. This knowledge allowed us to learn some exceptions such as *honor* and *amor*.

Something else stemming from this work was deciding what letters can signify more than one grammatical property; for example, *-o* can indicate first person singular, present tense, a nominative singular in third declension, a dative or ablative singular in second declension. All in all, these activities are fun for the students and rewarding with their abundance of knowledge. They also led to some excellent discussions for my own students.

Endings That Can Indicate More Than One Case

-a: nominative singular, first declension;
ablative singular, first declension;
nominative and accusative plural, second, third and fourth declension neuter nouns

-ae: genitive and dative singular, first declension;
nominative plural, first declension

-is: dative and ablative plural, first and second declensions;
genitive singular, third declension;
accusative plural, third declension

-us: nominative singular, first and fourth declensions;
genitive singular, fourth declension;
accusative plural, fourth declension

-i: genitive singular and nominative plural, second declension;
dative singular, third declension;
ablative singular, third declension neuter -i stems

-o: nominative singular, third declension;
dative and ablative singular, second declension

-um: nominative and accusative singular, second declension, neuter;
accusative singular, second declension, masculine;
genitive plural, third declension

-u: ablative singular, fourth declension;
nominative, dative, accusative, and ablative singular, fourth declension, neuter

-ibus: dative and ablative plural, third and fourth declensions

-es: nominative singular, nominative and accusative plural, fifth declension;
nominative and accusative plural, third declension

-ei: genitive and dative singular, fifth declension

-ebus: dative and ablative plural, fifth declension

-abus: dative and ablative plural, certain first declension nouns such as *fīlia* and *dea*

Third Declension Nominative Singular Final Letters

1.	**a**	(as in *drama*)
2.	**c**	(as in *lac*)
3.	**e**	(as in *mare*)
4.	**l**	(as in *consul*)
5.	**n**	(as in *flumen*)
6.	**o**	(as in *natio*)
7.	**r**	(as in *mater*)
8.	**s**	(as in *virtus*)
9.	**t**	(as in *caput*)
10.	**x**	(as in *rex*)

Selected Readings and Resources

Judith Lynn Sebesta

A full bibliography referencing all appropriate web sites, sources, etc., is impossible to keep current. The following items are listed as "gateway" sources that will enable teachers to obtain up-to-date information.

Internet Resources

Latin List — listserv@psuvm.psu.edu
In the body of the e-mail message, type "subscribe Latin-L"

American Classical League — a.c.l@umich.edu
In the body of the e-mail message, request to be added to the American Classical League announcement service.

Latin Night. American On Line: Tuesday night 7–8 p.m. (CDT)
A discussion group on classical topics especially for teachers. Contact:
LeaAnn Osburn, at Prof.Latin@aol.com
or Josephine Garmer, at MsMagistra@aol.com

World Wide Web Sites

The Campanian Society, Inc. organizes tours and offers tours of the classical world for teachers.
http://www.campanian.org

The Classics and Mediterranean Archaeological Homepage collects links to internet resources of interest to classicists and Mediterranean archaeologists.
http://rome.classics.lsa.umich.edu/welcome.html

Diotima offers sources (in translation), visuals, syllabi, articles, and more on women and gender in the ancient world, including the Near Eastern, Egyptian, Greek, Roman, Aegean, etc. cultures.
http://www.stoa.org/diotima

Electronic Resources for Classicists: The Second Generation has links to classics resources, journals, databases and web projects, bibliographies, images, course materials, and more.
http://www.tlg.uci.edu/~tlg/index/resources.html

Exploring Ancient World Cultures covers the ancient Near East, Rome, Greece, ancient India, ancient Egypt, early Islam, medieval Europe, and ancient China.
http://eawc.Evansville.edu

Greek Mythology Link has biographies of deities, heroes, etc.; geographical references, catalog of images, maps, and tables, all based on classical sources.
http://www.faunce2.brown.edu/~maicar/

Images of Women in Ancient Art: Issues of Interpretation and Identity provides images of women in prehistory, ancient Egypt, Greece, Palestine and the Aegean and barbarian women.

http://www.arthistory.sbc.edu/imageswomen/

Index Rerum Classicarum is dedicated to listing the classical material available on the World Wide Web and making it available to all students and teachers of ancient history, culture, civilization, and the classics. Topics include government and politics, art, archaeology, history, historical novels, and more.

http://www.geocities.com/Athens/Styx/9585/thingscl.html

The Latin Page is a page of general classroom aids designed primarily for the 7–12 Latin teacher. Some projects may be able to be adapted for lower grades with links to unique pages for Latin teaching and study.

http://www.geocities.com/Athens/Acropolis/3773/

Maecenas: Image of Ancient Greece and Rome is a searchable site of 1550+ images of Greece and Rome taken from the collection of Leo P. Curran. The images are downloadable and usable for any purpose except a commercial one.

http://wings.buffalo.edu/AandL/Maecenas/general_contents.html

The On-Line Encyclopedia of the Roman Provinces has articles about the Roman provinces written by scholars and refereed by the members of the ERP Editorial Board. The articles are updated as new archaeological information is acquired through excavation.

http://www.usd.edu/erp/

Ostia: The Harbour of Ancient Rome is dedicated to Ostia, the harbor of ancient Rome for professional archaeologists and historians, students of Roman archaeology and history, and interested lay-people. The site is maintained by the Internet Group Ostia (IGO).

http://www.ncl.ac.uk/ostia/

Perseus is an evolving digital library that covers the Greek and Roman world (and more). Classical resources include maps, images, dictionaries, texts and translations, encyclopedia articles and more. Images of Greek art and archaeology are available for purchase on CD-Rom.

http://www.perseus.tufts.edu

Promote Latin: The Web Page of the national Committee for Latin and Greek. The purpose of the NCLG is to initiate and coordinate efforts to promote the study of Latin and Greek on behalf of all cooperating classical associations by developing an agenda of promotional projects and activities. The web page contains news items, reasons for studying Latin and Greek, letters of support, promotional materials, placement services, and announcements.

http://www.promotelatin.org

Provinciae Imperii Romani is a developing site with an interactive map of the Roman provinces with short essays, written by college students, about each province.

http://www.usd.edu/~clehmann/pir/index.htm

Romulus Project is an electronic library of Latin literature with virtual commentary.

http://ccat.sas.upenn.edu/~romulus

The Stoa: A Consortium for Electronic Publication in the Humanities is a web page for electronic publication in the humanities with a special focus on the ancient world and the classical tradition.

http://www.stoa.org

Table of Contents of Journals of Interest to Classicists collects the tables of contents of a selection of about 160 Classics, Near Eastern Studies, and Religion journals, both in text format and through a Web search program. It also gives links (if possible) to articles of which the full text or an abstract is available online.

http://www.chass.utoronto.ca/amphoras/tocs.html

Virtual Tours provides online multimedia-guided tours of over 300 museums, exhibits, items of special interest, and real-time journeys. The site is particularly useful for teachers planning trips to these museums.

http://www.virtualfreesites.com/museums.html

Classical Organizations

Many states have their own state classics organization. Regional classical associations include: the Classical Association of New England, the Classical Association of the Atlantic States, the Classical Association of the Middle West and South (includes some Canadian provinces), the Classical Association of the Southwest United States, and the Classical Association of the Pacific Northwest. These associations have annual meetings, and several publish their own journals. The national classical association is The American Philological Association. Teachers may also be interested in the Archaeological Institute of America.

Current addresses for any of these associations may be obtained from The American Classical League, an association of elementary, middle school, and secondary school teachers, and college and university teachers of classical humanities and Latin and Greek. The ACL holds an annual institute with workshops, maintains a Teaching Materials and Resource Center and a National Teachers Placement Bureau, has scholarships for teachers, sponsors the National Latin Exam, and publishes *The Classical Outlook.*

The American Classical League
Miami University
Oxford, OH 45056
AmericanClassicalLeague@muohio.edu
http://www.aclclassics.org/
(513) 529-7741

Bibliographies

The Classical World, a journal published by the Classical Association of the Atlantic States, prints several surveys. The annual survey of Greek and Latin textbooks covers authors, beginner's textbooks, readers, grammars, dictionaries, etc., and also includes Medieval Latin and general vocabulary and medical vocabulary textbooks. Every two years *The Classical World* publishes an audio-visual materials survey that includes slides, movies, computer software, videos, etc. and a survey for books for teaching the classics in English. This survey is also available at www.drjclassics.com. For more information contact: The Classical Association of the Atlantic States, Department of Classics, Duquesne University, Pittsburgh, PA 15282-1704.

The following list of resources is selected from these surveys and other sources.

Software and CD-Rom

Artes Latinae: a self-paced, self-teaching Latin series, published by:

Bolchazy-Carducci Publishers
1000 Brown St. Unit 101
Wauconda, IL 60084
http://www.bolchazy.com

Centaur Systems publishes a number of tutorials, drills, games, and more, including Latin Vocabulary Drill that is keyed to various textbooks.

Centaur Systems Ltd.
407 N. Brearly St.
Madison, WI 53703
www.centaursystems.com

Perseus: Interactive Sources and Studies on Ancient Greece offers CD-Rom images of Greek art and archaeology, and site plans, etc. Order from Yale University Press.

Yale University Press
P.O. Box 209040
New Haven, CT 06520-9040
203/432-0960
http://www.yale.edu/yup/

S.P.Q.R.: The Empire's Darkest Hour: a mind-puzzling adventure game requiring knowledge of Latin and Roman culture and offering a 3-D reconstruction of ancient Rome, animations, movies.

GT Interactive Software Corporation
P.O. Box 3383
Redmond, WA 98052
http://www.gtstore.com

Transparent Language publishes several interactive, Latin learning and reference products.

Transparent Language, Inc.
9 Executive Park Drive
Merrimack, NH 03054
603-262-6300
http://www.TransparentLanguage.com
info@transparent.com

Vergil Reference CD-Rom contains the complete Latin and English texts, four complete reference works linked to the texts, note on the Latin and English texts, Latin-English dictionary, search guides, and teaching applications.

Paratext Inc.
1409 Newport Springs
Reston, VA 20194-1178
www.paratext.com/rrs

Periodicals

The following are journals of particular interest to middle school and secondary teachers of Latin and Classical Humanities.

The Classical Outlook is a journal for teachers that publishes articles, reports, instructional aids, poetry, reviews of software and textbooks, and other items of interest and use to classroom teachers of Latin, Greek, and Classical Humanities in elementary, middle, secondary schools and in colleges and universities. Contact:

The American Classical League
Miami University
Oxford, OH 45056
Email: AmericanClassicalLeague@muohio.edu
http://www.aclclassics.org/
(513) 529-7741

The New England Classical Journal is a journal for teachers that publishes articles, reports, instructional aids, poetry, reviews of software and textbooks, and other items of interest and use to classroom teachers of Latin, Greek, and Classical Humanities in elementary, middle, secondary schools and in colleges and universities. Contact:

William F. Wyatt, Editor-in-Chief
Box 1856
Brown University
Providence, RI 02912
NECN@brown.edu

Pompeiiana Newsletter is a newsletter in Latin for beginning and more advanced students of Latin, particularly in the middle and secondary schools, with news articles, puzzles, games, etc. Contact:

Pompeiiana, Inc.
6026 Indianola Avenue
Indianapolis, IN 46220-2014
http://www.pompeiiana.com

Calliope is a journal for students with articles in English on aspects of life in the ancient world. Contact:

Cobblestone Publishers
30 Grove Street
Peterborough, NH 03458
http://www.cobblestonepub.com

General Sources

The following provide various teaching materials such as tapes, CDs, buttons, maps, posters, slides, coins, stickers, mysteries set in antiquity, etc.

American Classical League Teaching Materials and Resource Center
Miami University
Oxford, OH 45056
AmericanClassicalLeague@muohio.edu
http://www.aclclassics.org/Resources/index.shtml
(513) 529-7741

Bolchazy-Carducci Publishers, Inc.
1000 Brown Street, Unit 101
Wauconda, IL 60084
http://www.bolchazy.com

The Campanian Society
Box 167
Oxford, OH 45056
http://www.campanian.org

L and L Enterprises
2408 Dawson Lane
Algonquin, IL 60102
LandL800@aol.com

Publishers

Teachers may find it useful to obtain catalogues from the following publishers who are major sources of books on classical culture and archaeology, classical texts, and authors. In addition, see the annual survey of textbooks for Latin and Greek and the audio-visual survey described above under "Bibliographies."

American Classical League Teaching Materials and Resource Center
Miami University
Oxford, OH 45056
AmericanClassicalLeague@muohio.edu
http://www.aclclassics.org/Resources/index.shtml
(513) 529-7741

Bolchazy-Carducci Publishers, Inc.
1000 Brown Street, Unit 101
Wauconda, IL 60084
http://www.bolchazy.com

Cambridge University Press
400 West 20th Street
New York, NY 10011-4211
http://www.cup.org

Caratzas, Aristide D., Publisher
Melissa International Publications, Ltd.
Caratzas/SVS Book Service
575 Scarsdale Road
Crestwood, NY 10707-1677
Phone: 800/204-2665, 914/961-2203
Fax: 914/961-5465

The Campanian Society
Box 167
Oxford, OH 45056
http://www.campanian.org

CANE Instructional Materials
71 Sand Hill Road
Amherst, MA 02001
http://www.wellesley.edu/ClassicalStudies/cane/cane.i.materials.html

Focus Publishing R. Pullins Co.
10 State Street, Box 369
Newbury Port, MA 01950
http://www.pullins.com

Oxford University Press
198 Madison Avenue
New York, NY 10016
http://www.oup.org

Latin Grammar & Composition

Gildersleeve's Latin Grammar
B.L. Gildersleeve & G. Lodge

The classic Latin grammar favored by many students and teachers with two new addtions:

✦ Foreword by **Ward W. Briggs, Jr.**

✦ Comprehensive bibliography by **William E. Wycislo.**

"Rightly interpreted, grammar is the culmination of philological study, and not its rudiment ... No study of literature can yield its highest result without the close study of language, and consequently the close study of grammar."

Basil L. Gildersleeve, *Selected Classical Papers*

"Compare his work with any other treatise hitherto in use, and its superiority will be manifest."

Southern Review

613 pp. (1895, third ed., reprint with additions 1997) paperback, ISBN 0-86516-353-7

New Latin Grammar
Charles E. Bennett

New Latin Grammar uses specific examples from primary sources to help students learn the inflections, syntax, sounds, accents, particles and word formations of the Latin language. It also includes a history of the Indo-European family of languages, the stages of the development of the Latin language and sections on prosody, the Roman calendar, Roman names, and definition and examples of figures of syntax and rhetoric.

xvi + 287 pp. (1908, Reprint 1995) paperback, ISBN 0-86516-261-1

New Latin Syntax
E. C. Woodcock

This book gives a historical account of the chief Latin constructions, aiming to equip students to interpret texts as well as to write correct Latin. The index of passages quoted makes it useful as a reference work for teachers. This is a necessary reference and an indispensable vademecum for teachers and advanced students.

xxiv + 267 pp. (1959, Reprint 1987) Paperback, ISBN 0-86516-126-7

New Latin Composition
Charles E. Bennett

In ***New Latin Composition,*** Bennett draws examples, vocabularies, and exercises from two of the most widely-read Latin authors: ✦ Caesar in Part I ✦ Cicero in Part II. Also includes sections on sentence composition, passage composition, oral composition, and the value of oral communication in Latin, which has only recently begun to be recognized.

ix + 292 pp. (1912, Reprint 1996) paperback, ISBN 0-86516-345-6

Latin Prose Composition & Key to Latin Prose Composition
M.A. North & A. E. Hillard

This book is aimed at helping students to enhance their command of Latin grammar and vocabulary with exercises structured in a manner that gradually enables students to build their Latin prose skills.

A book that has well stood the test of time. — **R. S. Kilpatrick,** Queen's University of Kingston

Latin Prose Composition: xix + 300 pp. (Reprint 1995), Paperback, ISBN 0-86516-308-1

Key to Latin Prose Composition: (Reprint 1996), Paperback, ISBN 0-86516-307-3

Graphic Latin Grammar
James P. Humphreys

Four double-sided pages containing all your Latin grammar charts on sturdy card stock ready for insertion in a 3-ring notebook.

(1961, Reprint 1995) Four 3-hole-punched laminated reference cards, ISBN 0-86516-111-1

BOLCHAZY-CARDUCCI Publishers, Inc.
orders@bolchazy.com

Latin References & Resources

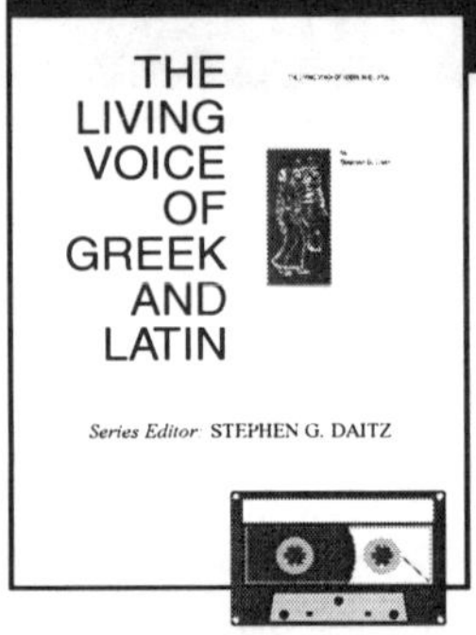

The Living Voice of Latin Literature
selections on cassettes read by STEPHEN G. DAITZ and ROBERT P. SONKOWSKY

THE PRONUNCIATION AND READING OF CLASSICAL LATIN: A Practical Guide, read by Stephen G. Daitz, Order #S23675

VERGIL: Selections, read by Robert P. Sonkowsky, Order #S23685

CICERO: Selections, read by Robert P. Sonkowsky, Order #S23680

CATULLUS AND HORACE: Selections, read by Robert P. Sonkowsky, Order #S23800

Each audio-lingual package consists of a booklet and two cassettes.

Why Vergil?
Stephanie Quinn

A collection of essays with bibliography to help understand and appreciate this great Latin epic better. A "must" for AP teachers. Available 1998.

A Handbook of Latin Literature
From the earliest times to the death of St. Augustine
H. G. Rose

This reference work offers a matchless overview of Latin literature. Also included is a supplementary bibliography by E. Courtney.

582 pp. (1936, rpt. 1996), Paperback, ISBN: 0-86516-317-0

The Comic History of Rome
Gilbert Abbott A Beckett, illustrated by John Leech

Beckett's *The Comic History of Rome*, first published in London in 1852, is now available in a reprint. The author's intent is to combine **instruction** with **amusement**. Teachers and students alike will welcome Beckett's humor and witty representation of the great chapters of Roman history from the earliest times to the death of Caesar.

100 + illustrations, xii, 308 p. (1852, rpt. 1996), Paperback, ISBN: 0-86516-333-2

A Short Guide to Classical Mythology
G. M. Kirkwood

Kirkwood's text provides a user-friendly, quick reference guide for teachers, students and general readers. It is an excellent, interdisciplinary resource beneficial in the study of classics, literature and history. This edition, with entries of variable length, features:

✦ pronunciation ✦ principal stories of classical mythology ✦ emphasis on literary importance of Greek myths ✦ references to English and European literature.

120 pp. (1959, Reprint 1995), Paperback, ISBN 0-86516-309-X

Elementary Latin Translation: Latin Readings for Review
A. E. Hillard and C. G. Botting, eds., with additions by Donald H. Hoffman

This graded reader is an excellent supplement to first-year Latin texts or as a review tool. The Latin is pure, simple, idiomatic, and easily understood by beginning students. Each review features two readings that acquaint the student with the chief events of Roman history and stories from Greek mythology. Latin references eliminate the need to consult other grammars.

vii + 192 pp. (1961, Reprint 1997), Paperback, ISBN 0-86516-403-7

BOLCHAZY-CARDUCCI Publishers, Inc.
http://www.bolchazy.com

Latin in Music

—Sine musica nulla disciplina potest esse perfecta; nihil enim est sine illa.—

Vergil's Dido and Mimus Magicus

New

composed by Jan Novák

conducted by Rafael Kubelik

An oratorio of two famous Vergil passages: *Dido,* taken from the fourth book of the *Aeneid;* and *Mimus Magicus,* from Vergil's eighth *Eclogue* on **CD**. Includes a libretto in Latin, English, and German. New import to America. Originally recorded by *audite* Schallplatten, Ostfildern, Germany, 1986.

Limited Edition CD (1997), 40-page libretto in Latin, English and German, ISBN 0-86516-346-4

Schola Cantans

New

composed by Jan Novák

A **cassette** with musical arrangement of ***Catullus*** (34) Dianae Sumus in Fide; ***Catullus*** (5) Vivamus Mea Lesbia; ***Catullus*** (61) Collis O Heliconii; ***Horace*** (Carm. I.22) Integer Vitae; ***Horace*** (Carm. I.2) Iam Satis Terris; ***Horace*** (Epod. 15) Nox Erat; Gaudeamus Igitur; Nautarum Carmen; ***Caesar*** (BG I.1-3) Gallia Est Omnis Divisa; ***Carmina Burana*** (142) Tempus Adest Floridum; ***Carmina Burana*** (85) Veris Dulcis in Tempore; ***Phaedrus*** (I.13) Vulpis et Corvus; and ***Martial*** (62) Ludi Magister.

Cassette: (1998) ISBN 0-86516-357-X
Music Score: (1998) ISBN 0-86516-358-8
Cassette and Music Score Set: (1998) ISBN 0-86516-404-5

Latin Music Through the Ages

Cynthia Kaldis

The illustrated book includes the Latin text, English translation, vocabulary, essays, and bibliography to accompany the musical performance. The seventeen Latin songs are directed by Clayton Lein and sung by the Lafayette Chamber Singers.

Book: Illus., xli + 87 pp. (1991) Paperback, ISBN 0-86516-242-5
Cassette: ISBN 0-86516-249-2

Latine Cantemus: Cantica Popularia Latine Reddita

Franz Schlosser, *trans. and illus.*

This illustrated edition features ✦ 60 new Latin translations ✦ traditional Latin favorites ✦ Christmas songs ✦ well-known Gregorian chants.

Illus., vii + 135 pp. (1996), Paperback, ISBN 0-86516-315-4

Carmina Burana

Judith Sebesta

Carl Orff's selections of twenty-four "*cantiones profanae*" from the Middle Ages are explored in this illustrated, dual-language edition featuring the original Latin poems with facing translations and vocabulary, complete vocabulary, bibliography, and study materials. Also included is a literary translation by Jeffrey M. Duban. In addition to medieval woodcutes, this new edition contains seventeen original illustrations by Thom Kapheim.

Illus. 165 pp. (Enhanced reprint 1996), Paperback, ISBN 0-86516-268-9

"Yes, Virginia, there is a Santa Claus" ... in Latin
Vere, Virginia, Sanctus Nicolaus est!

"Please tell me the truth, is there a Santa Claus?" On September 21, 1897, the minds and hearts of two people met and in that meeting created magic that has survived more than a century. VIRGINIA O'HANLON's earnest question set New York Sun editor FRANCIS PHARCELLUS CHURCH to writing. Church's reply, a testimony to the existence of Santa Claus, on the marvels of the unseen but very real world of wonder, are now a part of Christmas lore. This edition offers a translation into Latin of the text of Church's well-known editorial. The Latin text is handsomely scripted and charmingly illustrated.

Significant Features
✦ New Latin translation, in ornate script with decorated capitals
✦ All new, full-color, charming illustrations for the Latin text
✦ English text on dual-language (English-Latin) pages in easy-to-read type, to aid translation of Latin
✦ Full Latin-English glossary
✦ "Christmas Memories" journal pages

32 pp. (2001) Hardbound, ISBN 0-86516-506-8

Cattus Petasatus: The Cat in the Hat in Latin

One of the first books for countless children, this story of a free-spirited Cat who, with his high jinks and mischievous friends (Things One and Two) turns the house upside-down for two bored children on a rainy day—is retold in Latin in Cattus Petasatus. This edition features the original artwork of Dr. Seuss and a translation in rhyming verse that echoes the sound of the original Cat in the Hat.

Significant Features
✦ Original artwork of Dr. Seuss ✦ Latin-to-English vocabulary ✦ Note on the verse-form and rhythm

80 pp. (2000) Paperback, ISBN 0-86516-472-X; Hardbound, ISBN 0-86516-471-1

Quomodo invidiosulus nomine GRINCHUS Christi natalem abrogaverit How the Grinch Stole Christmas in Latin

The timeless tale of how the true spirit of Christmas captured the heart of the irascible Grinch is retold in Latin in Quomodo invidiosulus nomine GRINCHUS Christi natalem abrogaverit. This edition features the original artwork of Dr. Seuss and a translation that echoes the word play and rhythmic narrative of the world's best-selling children's author.

Significant Features
✦ Original artwork of Dr. Seuss ✦ Latin-to-English vocabulary
✦ Note on the translation

Seven years after his death in 1991, Dr. Seuss — pen name for Theodor Geisel — continues to be the best-selling children's author in the world. Seuss, who understood the serious nature of whimsy, offered beginning readers a fanciful alternative to the mundane world of Dick and Jane. Although he is best known for his innovative approach to children's literature, Seuss won two academy awards for best documentary and was a talented political satirist.

64 pp. (1998) Paperback, ISBN 0-86516-420-7; Hardbound, ISBN 0-86516-419-3

The Wisdom of the Ancients on Latin Buttons

B1 Amat victoria curam. (Anon.) Victory likes careful preparation.
B2 Experientia docet. (Tacitus) Experience teaches.
B3 Urbes constituit aetas, hora dissolvit. (Anon.) A period of time builds up cities, a single hour destroys them.
B4 Modus omnibus in rebus. (Plautus) Moderation in all things.
B5 Saepe summa ingenia in occulto latent. (Plautus) Often the greatest minds lie hidden.
B6 Ipsa scientia potestas est. (Sir Francis Bacon?) Knowledge itself is power.
B7 Non est ad astra mollis e terris via. (Seneca) The trip from the earth to the stars is not an easy one.
B8 Longum iter est per praecepta, breve et efficax per exempla. (Seneca) The journey is long through advice, but short and efficient through examples.
B9 Nihil est...simul et inventum et perfectum. (Cicero) Nothing is simultaneously both conceived and perfected.
B10 Damnant quod non intellegunt. (Anon.) They condemn what they do not understand.
B11 Errare est humanum. (Anon.) To err is human.
B12 Mens sana in corpore sano. (Juvenal) A sound mind in a sound body.
B13 Ars longa, vita brevis. (Hippocrates-translation) Art is long, life is short.
B14 Cogito, ergo sum. (Descartes-translation) I think, therefore I am.
B15 Sed quis custodiet ipsos custodes? (Juvenal) But who will watch the custodians themselves?
B16 Veni, vidi, vici. (Suetonius) I came, I saw, I conquered.
B17 Virtus et sapientia. (Anon.) Virtue and wisdom.
B18 Dabit deus his quoque finem. (Vergil) God will also give an end to these things.
B19 Timeo Danaos et dona ferentis. (Vergil) I fear Greeks (even) bearing gifts.
B20 Citius Altius Fortius. (Olympics Motto) Faster, Higher, Stonger.
B21 Forsan et haec olim meminisse juvabit. (Vergil) Perhaps some day it will bring pleasure to remember even these things.
B22 Quod licet Jovi non licet bovi. (Anon.) What is permitted to Jupiter is not permitted to the ox.
B23 Divide et impera. (Anon.) Divide and conquer.
B24 Ego sum rex Romanus et supra grammaticam. (King Sigismund the First?) I am a Roman king and above grammar.
B25 Homo sum; humani nil a me alienum puto. (Terence) I am a human being; I consider nothing human alien to me.
B26 Spem successus alit. (Anon.) Success feeds hope.
B27 Non omnis moriar. (Horace) Not all of me shall die.
B28 Roma Alma Mater. (Anon) Rome, our nourishing mother.

Buttons are $1.50 each and orders must have a minimum of 15 buttons.
You can order fewer than 15 buttons if ordered with other items in our catalog.
NOTE: Buttons do not have the English translations on them.

Bolchazy-Carducci Publishers, Inc.
1000 Brown St., Unit 101
Wauconda, IL 60084 USA
(847) 526-4344; *Fax:* (847) 526-2867
www.bolchazy.com

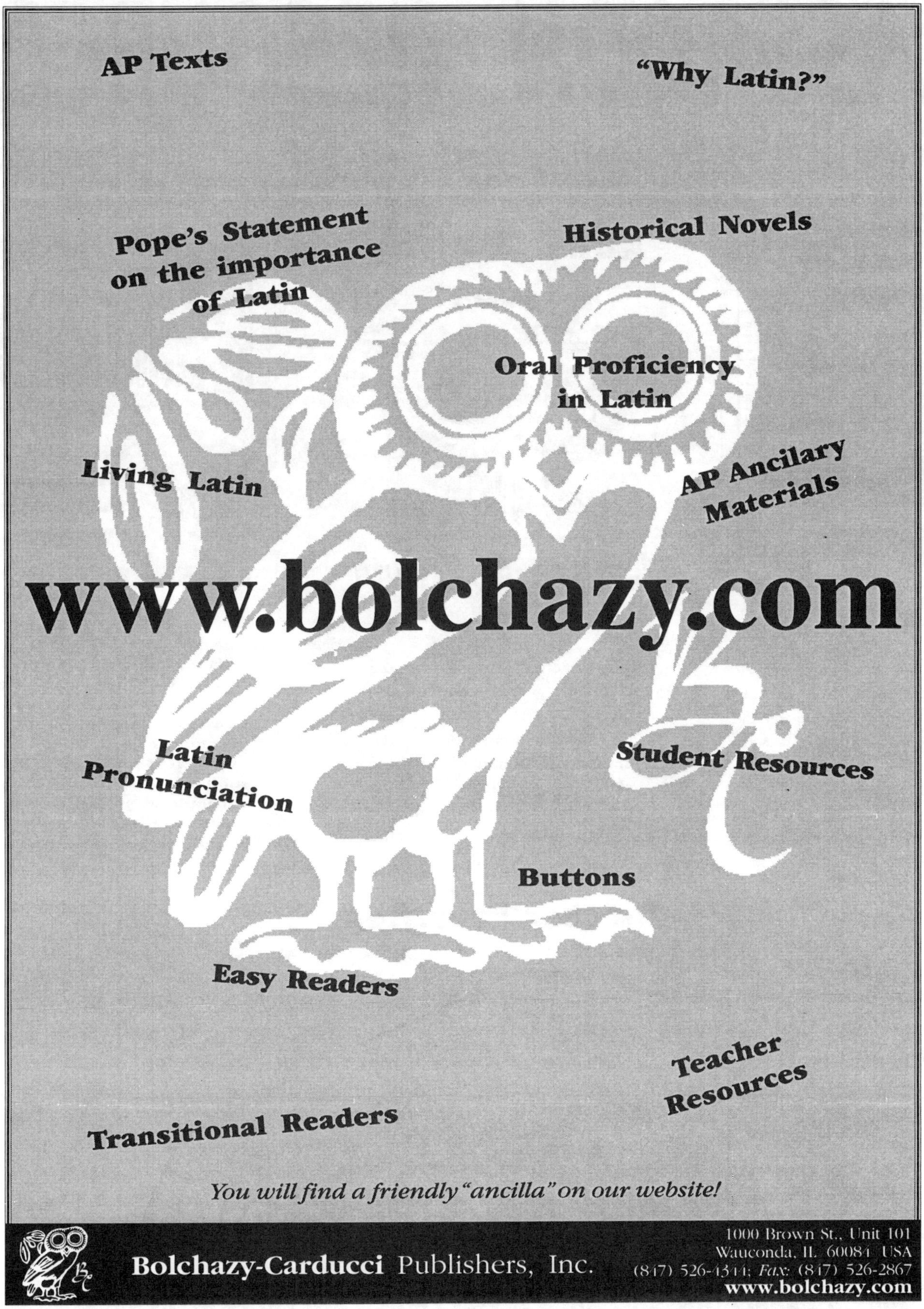
AP Texts
"Why Latin?"
Pope's Statement on the importance of Latin
Historical Novels
Oral Proficiency in Latin
Living Latin
AP Ancilary Materials
www.bolchazy.com
Latin Pronunciation
Student Resources
Buttons
Easy Readers
Teacher Resources
Transitional Readers
You will find a friendly "ancilla" on our website!
Bolchazy-Carducci Publishers, Inc.
1000 Brown St., Unit 101
Wauconda, IL 60084 USA
(847) 526-4344; Fax: (847) 526-2867
www.bolchazy.com

THE CLASSICAL ASSOCIATION OF NEW ENGLAND (CANE)
The professional organization for teachers of Latin, Greek, and the Classics in New England

New England Classical Journal: All CANE members receive the Association's quarterly journal featuring professional articles, aids for teachers, and book reviews, as well as CANE's current news and activities.

CANE Summer Institute: lectures, mini-courses, discussions, and fellowship at Dartmouth College each summer.

CANE Resources
*__Computer Resources:__ programs, computing advice, and Home Page.
* **CANE's Video Lending Library** offers CANE members a wide selection of titles at minimal cost.
* **Classics-in-Crisis** is a professional resource support for classics programs in difficulty.
* **CANE Instructional Materials** publishes extensive resources for teaching the Classics at all levels.
* **Emporium Romanum** provides a selection of items featuring classical languages and art.
* **New England Latin Placement Service** provides information on positions in middle and secondary schools.

CANE's **annual Writing Contest** is open to middle- and secondary-school students of CANE members.

CANE Annual Meeting, a professional and social gathering of members from schools, colleges, and universities.

CANE Scholarships and Grants
* **The Cornelia Catlin Coulter Memorial Scholarship** for summer study at the American academy in Rome.
* **The CANE Endowment Scholarship** supports other programs of summer study in the Classics.
* **Discretionary grants** of up to $200 are available for specific pedagogical or research projects.
* **The Renata Poggioli Award**, offered in alternate years, funds travel in Greece and Italy.

For a membership application write CANE's Treasurer, Ruth Breindel, Moses Brown School, 250 Lloyd Avenue, Providence, RI 02906. http://www.caneweb.org